Jeffries Wyman

Letters from Japan 1950

Transcribed from handwritten letters
by his daughter, Anne Cabot Wyman

Wash drawings and map by Julia Blackbourn

Open Book Systems, Inc. / Protean Press
37-J Whistlestop Mall
Rockport, MA 01966
www.ProteanPress.com

14 13 12 11 10   2 3 4 5

Library of Congress Cataloging-in-Publication Data
Wyman, Jeffries, 1901–1995.
Letters from Japan 1950 / Jeffries Wyman ; transcribed from handwritten letters
by his daughter, Anne Cabot Wyman ; wash drawings and map by Julia Blackbourn.
p. cm.
Previously published: 2000.
ISBN 978-0-9625780-6-9
1. Japan—Description and travel. 2. Wyman, Jeffries, 1901-1995—Correspondence.
I. Wyman, Anne Cabot. II. Blackbourn, Julia. III. Title. IV. Title: Jeffries Wyman
letters from Japan 1950.
DS811.W96 2010
952.04'5092—dc22

2009024296

Manufactured in the United States of America by Fleming Printing Company
40 White Street, Somerville, Massachusetts

For J.W.'s friends

Kyoshi Kurahashi and Yoshiaki Miura

and in memory of Ichiro Mizushima

Table of Contents

Introduction

A Harvard biochemist, Jeffries Wyman set out in June, 1950 to give a series of scientific lectures in Korea and was enroute there when the Korean War broke out. Instead, he spent six months in General Douglas MacArthur's post-war Japan. His view is that of an adventurer and enthusiast.

Then aged 49 and very energetic, my father was warmly welcomed by the Allied Forces, who were rebuilding the country's infrastructure, and by Japan's academic community. But his warmest connections were always with the fishermen, villagers and members of Japan's old aristocracy, whom he sought out on long treks on foot and by small boats in the countryside.

Emperor Hirohito, a fellow biologist, received him on his second day in Japan. The Emperor's master of ceremonies, the Marquis of Matsudira, invited him to dinner and became a friend. In the north island of Hokkaido, Jeffries walked over a high pass in a national forest, accompanied by a member of the Sapporo University football team and a forest ranger armed with a gun against bears. In August, he spent the better part of a week on the large feudal farm of the Count Hirata, an eccentric painter and poet whose father had been chancellor to the previous emperor.

"Farmy's" detailed accounts of food, art and local customs are accompanied by romantic and occasionally hyperbolic commentary. Voyaging by propeller boat up a mountain river south of Kyoto, Jeffries was "deeply humiliated" to pass a fleet of local craft traveling under sail "like a company of nymphs." Included are also personal notes on family matters in Boston and on the world scene.

The letters to me and my brother, Jeff, both then in college, were all hand written, usually in pencil, and often on both sides of durable but highly transparent Japanese paper. I have transcribed them verbatim except for corrections in spelling and bracketed inserts for clarification.

Anne Cabot Wyman
Cambridge, Massachusetts
September, 1999

Places in order of appearance
(Japan has 4 islands: Hokkaido, Honshu,
Shikoku and Kyushu)

- Tokyo
  Hakone
  Chiba Peninsula
  Kamakura
  Nikko

- Aomori (northern port, Honshu)
  Hakodate (southern port, Hokkaido)
  Sapporo (capital of Hokkaido)
  Samani (southeast of Sapporo on Pacific)
  Obihiro
  Kushiro

- Sendai (Pacific Coast north of Tokyo)
  Nasu (between Tokyo and Sendai)

- Niigata (west coast of Honshu)
  Sado Island
  Kanazawa

- Nagoya (south of Kanazawa)
  Ise (south of Nagoya)

- Numazu (south of Mt. Fuji)
  Suzenji (south of Mt. Fuji)

- Kyoto (old capital, west of Tokyo)
  Nara (site of typhoon)
  Osaka (south of Kyoto)

- Kii Peninsula (south of Nara)
  Shingu
  Kii Peninsula
  Kumano River
  Nachi-Katsuura

- Fukuoka (air-base for Korea)

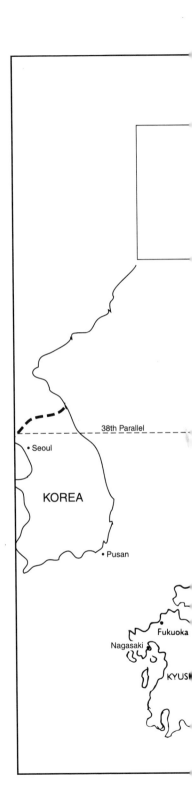

Map of Japan

circa 1950

N

SEA OF JAPAN

HOKKAIDO

Sapporo • Obihiro • Kushiro •

Samani

Hakodate

Aomori •

Sendai • 38°

Sado Island • Niigata

• Nasu

• Nikko

• Kanazawa

HONSHU Tokyo ◉

★ Mt. Fuji

Kyoto Nagoya Hakone • Chiba Peninsula

Osaka Numazu • Kamakura

iroshima • Nara Suzenji

Ise •

Kumano River

SHIKOKU Shingu • Kii Peninsula

Nachi-Katsuura

PACIFIC OCEAN

Letters from Japan

Dear Anne & Jeff, I have been in a kind of dream world for the last 36 hours. When I last wrote to you we were just approaching Semya, one of the outermost Aleutians. Such a gray barren place, covered with runways and empty barracks, as it turned out to be! And cold. There were on the plane: 2 Japanese, one Korean, 4 women headed for Seoul to join US husbands & fathers, a Northwest Airlines man bound to Okinawa, and a young boy to be dropped off at Semya.

We were met by a dilapidated bus and hurried up to a little barracks building where tea, coffee, cut up fruit & sandwiches were waiting for us. Through the haze, we could see the towering headland of a nearby island, quite different from ours. There we all sat, talking & drinking coffee, & waiting for the reconditioning of our plane, which was by now half full of freight. We had already had word of the war in Korea & knew that all plane service from Tokyo to Korea had been abandoned.

By and by we were rattled down the hill in the bus and boarded the plane and took off into the murky darkness of the N. Pacific. I went to sleep almost at once, as I find it easy to do in a plane. But the night was long and we had to set our watches back & back. The dawn came up very slowly for we were flying pretty much straight away from the sun, and it was some time after dawn that the clouds began to break just as we came upon one of the most beautiful landfalls I have ever seen. It was really the world of the Japanese painters that lay below us. Our approach was over the east coast, about 330 miles N of Tokyo, where there is quite a point that juts out into the Pacific. The big swells were breaking on it. Everything was incredibly green, about the color of malachite, and the land was quite heavily wooded with a few neatly tilled fields lying together here &

there. You could see the little roads and paths running over the ground and here and there groups of low farm buildings.

As we flew south, paralleling the shore, the country became on the whole steadily less mountainous and the exactly rectangular rice paddies & other fields covered a larger & larger part of the land. We crossed many rivers, ditches & canals, the lesser ones spanned by bridges. Finally we found ourselves over the great open plain, coming down from the NW to Tokyo Bay and we could see the vast pall of smoke covering the great city. Tokyo has 6,000,000 inhabitants. Steamers were lying in the roadsted and, near the shores of the bay where the water was shallow, were many fish traps of various shapes. Fishermen were sculling themselves about in ancient looking boats & there were a few motor boats.

Soon we were on the field and through Customs. There was considerable confusion due to events in Korea. Of course I was planning to stay in Japan for a few days anyway but, for the 5 regular through passengers for Seoul, it was all most upsetting. I had a note to call Col. [Laurence] Bunker, Gen. MacA's [Douglas MacArthur's] aide-de-camp, which I did before getting hotel accomodations. The long rough bus trip from the airport to the centre of town was through a new world. Men & women all of a new race hurrying here & there, some in kimonos, more in American dress, many of the women with babies strapped to their backs, a large number of the people barefoot, with sandals, or wearing clogs.

I finally arranged for a billet through the military billeting office in a very comfortable family hotel mainly occupied by the Australian military and their families but with some Americans. After a shower, a change of clothes & a good breakfast, I got into a cab & drove over to G.H.Q. to see Bunker. From him I discovered that the Reds had penetrated deep into Korea and, although everything was very uncertain, it was fairly clear that there could be no thought of going on to Korea for some weeks, in all probability. So I have been thinking of changing plans to stay in Japan. But nothing is clear so far.

I was almost sorry not to have been in Korea to see something of the shooting war, but I suppose I should have only been packed off to the South and evacuated to Japan along with the other Westerners, after excruciating delays in this humid heat.

To my great surprise, I discovered that the Emperor had heard of my coming through one of his aides via Col. Bunker & had expressed a desire to see me, and that an audience had been arranged for this morning (my second day.) I was of course much thrilled at the thought of it as I stood in the windows of the G.H.Q. and looked over the expanse of green — over 200 acres — of the palace grounds beyond the great moats and colossal granite walls that surround them. In the meantime, a certain young Nisei lieutenant was delegated to work out my schedule.

I had lunch with an American fisheries man who us here with SCAP [Supreme Command Allied Powers] helping reorganize the Japanese industry. I met his boss, Col. Schenk, who was a good-natured bluff man who asked me to dinner tomorrow. After lunch I went to see the Imperial collection of art under the direction of Dr. Harada, who is a friend of L[angdon] Warner. He is a delightful, kindly old man with quite a twinkle who showed me over his superb possessions.

Then a jeep from G.H.Q. whirled me back to the hotel where I received a call from a man named Saito with his wife and daughter. I gather he is quite swell, being a son (adopted according to ▓▓ custom) of the admiral who was Gov. General of Korea and then Prime Minister and was finally murdered — for his virtues, for he was a very fine man. Saito is a member of the House of Lords but is also an official of a big insurance company. His wife was a great lady, as it was easy to see, and came dressed in a kimono with a fan. Then a most awkward thing happened, which I shall never forget or forgive. I took them into the hotel lounge for cocktails only to have the wretched Cockney hotel manager — as I say, this hotel has been taken over by the Australians — call me aside to say that ▓▓▓ were absolutely prohibited from the hotel. It was most embarrassing but we went off to his office for a good talk & there I was offered sherbet & iced coffee in a tower room overlooking the vast city.

When I expressed an interest in the Japanese theater, they said they would take me to one, and soon afterwards I found myself with them all in the front box, which seemed to open like magic as the attendant bent almost to the ground while we entered. All the players were men, though some, of course, took the part of women. There was an intermittent noise produced by the beating of wooden sticks beforehand and throughout the play. When the curtain went up, or rather, aside, for it was pushed open by an old man running across the stage, there were no actors to be seen. The setting was that of a Buddhist temple. The actors finally entered down a long walk at the side, painted or powdered white, and they looked exactly like the pictures of actors and geisha girls that you see in Japanese prints and kakemonos. Their voices were harsh and shrill. We sat fanning ourselves — I had been provided with a fan — as we watched. There were several plays which were little love scenes and intrigues. Saito explained it all to me as it went on, though his English leaves something to be desired. The last play was really a dance, of extraordinary beauty and great feeling, in spite of the rigid and artificial conventions (from our point of view). It ended with the dancer, a beautiful young "girl" standing by the huge temple bell in which was concealed the young priest she was in love with but who was hiding from her.

Between the acts we went out and had iced drinks. After it was all over I took the Saitos to supper at a little restaurant of their choosing. While we were sitting there, a quite informally dressed man came up to speak to us, and to my astonishment, he was the Empress's brother! By now, my eyes were heavy after the long trip in the plane and the heat and humidity of my first day, so I was glad to be dropped at my hotel and say good night.

Next Day: I am resuming this on Thursday. It was so sultry and hot that I waked very early next day and was glad to have a cool shower before breakfast. This was to be my big morning when I was to be called for by Dr. Tagami and escorted to the palace. But after breakfast I had a call from Dr. Kamayama, president of the Japanese Council of Science, whom I had met last spring in U.S.A. He is to call again this afternoon.

I was to be called for at precisely 10:15 by my escort and he came, punctual to the dot, with a car and a driver from G.H.Q. It was quite thrilling to drive past the guards at the Palace gate, over the bridge over the moat. At one point, there is a very beautiful double bridge but that is not the one we took. The main old palace was burned in the war and the Emperor lives in a modern stone palace (the old one was wood) of European design which was formerly for the household offices. Our car had a great red emblem stuck to the windshield to show that we were going to the Emperor's. As we drew up at the porte-cochere, various flunkies came forward and then the Emperor's interpreter in cut-away coat and striped trousers as well as some other household official whose name I never did get. We were taken up a long flight of stairs and into an immense waiting room of European character but with some large screens and vases and with furniture upholstered in magnificent Japanese brocade.

Now came in the Marquis of Matsudaira, the master of ceremonies, a ghostly thin little man in a cutaway coat who had been at Oxford. Next a roly-poly man who is the grand chamberlain, and who had been the Japanese ambassador at Vichy. We sat and talked politely until the exact moment should arrive. Then I was escorted down another long corridor past bowing flunkies and shown into an audience room with some very large handsome screens and gold furniture. Here we all sat rather stiffly until the great moment of the Emperor's entering, which he did very simply and modestly, dressed in a light-colored European suit just like mine. He looks like his pictures, short, unimpressive, rather stocky, with spectacles. He shook hands and bade me sit down. The interpreter was a little nervous. It seems that the Emperor is much interested in Biology and Natural History, and does a great deal of collecting of invertebrate animals near his summer palace at Sagami Bay.

I had been presented with a sumptuously illustrated book describing some of the new species of mollusks which he had collected; so after a few exchanges of compliments, we began talking of biology. He wanted to hear about my activities and was really much interested, but it was too hard for the poor interpreter, who was an extremely nice man knowing nothing of science. I felt at first stiff and constrained, partly by the sitting and partly by having to depend on the interpreter. The Emperor never looked at the interpreter but always at me, and I kept turning towards the interpreter as I replied, which I suppose is a mistake. But it was a very nice, easy conversation in the end, which made me feel that in the Emperor I was dealing with a simple, friendly man whom I liked instinctively better than anyone else in the room, with the possible exception of the interpreter.

We talked half an hour or more until the Emperor terminated the interview with some compliments to which I replied as best I could. He asked me if I would like to see his laboratory and regretted that he could not go with me. He was about to receive the new prime minister who was forming a cabinet and was waiting. He entered as I left.

The interpreter then took me and my escort through the palace grounds — very beautiful and deeply wooded — past an ancestral shrine which we alighted to look at, and up to the laboratory building where they were waiting for us. After a tour there, I was asked whether I would not like to see the famous stables. Of course I said Yes and there, sure enough, was the Emperor's famous white horse — very mild and good mannered I am sure. Next him was one very like, belonging to the crown prince. All the horses were in large box stalls. Next we went to see the imperial carriages and state coaches. There was a magnificent lacquered ceremonial saddle with trappings all in the Japanese manner, which interested me greatly, but the carriages were all in the European style. After that, I was taken to the riding pavillion where the horses were trained and exercised, but unfortunately all the boys were at lunch hour, playing baseball in the yard, & no one was riding. Then we paid a final visit to see the Emperor's automobile, with its gilded ornaments, but much inferior to the carriages, and so home.

The whole thing took about 2 1/2 hours and is something I shall never forget. It was unexpected that I should carry away such a strong feeling for the Emperor's warm, simple personality. I should really like to know him. Poor man, he is the prisoner of his household ceremonies. He lives, I am told, in a little house deep in the woods of his park, and not at all in his palace. It is like the Tale of Genji, adapted to modern times. Matsudaira, the master of ceremonies is the father (adopted) of his brother's wife, the Princess Chichibu. As we left the palace gates, the red emblem on our windshield was removed.

In the afternoon I went to see the university, a rather dingy place where I was shown over the laboratories. I was received by the dean & then taken over to the biologists who were all sitting round a big table where I was given tea. When I got back I had a call from a friend of Saito's, named Matsumoto, who had visited Harvard. We went out for a bottle of beer & I had a pleasant talk with him. But I was ready for a bath & a nap before Bunker's car called for me at 8 to take me out to dinner at his luxurious quarters adjoining MacArthur's at the Embassy.

We dined alone together, for he is a bachelor. He has a very fine chef, who was chef for one of the princes, and a most exquisite little maid who was dressed in a kimono and moved about noiselessly, filling our glasses and plying us with food. But I should not like his job — always on call, the centre of all the complications and having to make innumerable minor decisions with no power to make the important ones. I stayed till 11:30 & then was driven home luxuriously in the G.H.Q. car.

There is really great composure here about Korea — much interest but no excitement. The general feeling seems to be that, if we do not preserve S. Korea, our prestige will be shattered past repair in Japan, and I should think that must be so. It remains to be seen what will happen.

I am expecting to go over to see Mr. Sebold, the ambassador, later this morning to talk about prospects & the possibility of adapting my plans to a stay in Japan if Korea remains inaccessible, as I believe it will for some time. Then I shall see Dr. Kamayama, and after that Baron Dan, the great art figure, to whom I have a letter from L[angdon] Warner & through whom I hope to see some of the private collections. This evening, as I told you, I am going to dinner with Col. Schenk.

I am getting very impatient with Tokyo and long to get out of it. It is hot, noisy and terribly westernized. I would love to get a guide and go to the most out-of-the-way parts of Japan and walk through the hills & paint & stay with the people. But I also want to see Kyoto & Nara & Nikko.

No more now. Yr devoted Farmy

After lunch, waiting for Kamayama: I may as well fill this sheet since I shall have to send it blank otherwise. I have had a talk with Sebold who seems to think some arrangement may be made to use my services here in Japan. It would be nice to spend a while at each of their universities. I am going to have another talk about it all tomorrow. It seems to be impossible to get out of Tokyo just yet.

I gather from Sebold that the problem of looking out for all the Korean evacuees, now in the south on the island of Kyushu, is causing him great trouble. It is certainly well that all this happened before I got there. Most of them have had to leave nearly all their personal belongings behind & must be destitute of money. What a mad world it is.

I do not know how best to tell you to reach me. I am of course most anxious to have news of home. You can, until a more permanent address is available, reach me

c/o Col. Laurence Bunker
General Headquarters
Office of the Supreme Commander for the Allied Powers
Tokyo
c/o Postmaster, San Francisco

I greatly want to hear how you, Anne, got on with [Dean] Kirby Miller [of Radcliffe College] & what you are going to do.

July 3, 1950 (postmarked July 6)   *Bath at Hakone*
                                              JW in Tokyo to Milton, MA

Dear Anne & Jeff, I am still here in Tokyo while things are so upset in Korea & it is very uncertain when I shall get there. Japan is full of refugees. I am hoping to arrange for a round of visits to the various Japanese universities to occupy the next month or several months until things get straightened out (if they ever do.) This, which I may have spoken of in my last letter, is being handled by Dr. Kamayama, Pres. of the Japanese Science Council, and Brig. [John] O'Brien, an Australian who is in the science & research section of SCAP (That is the abbreviation for Supreme Commander, Allied Powers). There is to be a meeting about it tomorrow afternoon and I shall know better what to expect after that. In the meantime, I am seeing something of Japan and Japanese life, though Tokyo is not the best place to do it.

It is a huge city, some say the 3rd largest in the world, and I should suppose that, if Yokahama were reckoned in, which is after all completely contiguous with it, that it must easily be so. It is in many ways much westernized with cars, buses & trains. But one sees much that is uniquely Japanese about it all the same. A large part of it consists of the flimsiest of little match-stick houses, which must be insupportably cold in winter, but there are of course some very fine houses.

I went to lunch at the O'Briens' house the other day. He being a Brig. General has one of the fine houses, which has been commandeered from the owner who was a great industrialist. The latter & his family live in a little building at the back of the garden. The house is charming with spacious open rooms looking out on a 3 acre garden with trees & stone monuments. O'B has a staff of 9 to look after the place. It all must cost virtually nothing to him and, as for food, it is to be had at much reduced prices in government commissaries. Gasoline here is 12-14 cents a gallon. There is a famous remark of one of the occupying people who said "We never had it so good before."

The Japanese themselves are kept in a very subordinate position, even those of high rank. They are all very poor, for there was a 90% capital levy which applied even to the Emperor. American drivers feel quite free to pass the traffic signals and are of course wholly independent of Japanese police. I do not know that the state of affairs is good for either side. But I believe MacArthur is very popular and certainly his administration is a remarkable achievement. He is really a new Shogun and the country sees the renewal of a relation between Emperor and governing power which they enjoyed for centuries up to about 1870. But of course the fact that it is all foreign, and results from defeat and occupation, makes a great difference.

I had another dinner, other than that with Bunker, with Col. Schenk, who also has a fine Jap. house & garden, though a simpler one than O'Brien's. His wife is with him, and he also has a very attractive woman [guest] who was born in Japan of Swiss father and American mother, & is now administering U.N. aid to Japanese children. She travels much about the country. The number of children, I may say, that one sees is enormous and the population of the country is greater by some millions than it was before the war.

The other evening I had a call from a Japanese Samurai, a friend of Saito's, named Matsumoto. He is a curious and amusing fellow who was at Oxford & has visited Harvard. He was with the group that represented the Emperor at the British coronation. I have had dinner with him twice since in Japanese restaurants. The first was a regular restaurant, where we had an elaborate meal of many courses accompanied by sake. It is most difficult for me to eat with chopsticks but I

am learning. It is the custom to bring a hot wet napkin to each guest with which he can wipe both hands and mouth. While we ate, the girls of the place come to converse with us and entertain us, which they did very nicely according to Japanese custom. The second meal was last evening at a little "diner," a tiny wooden affair on wheels which is brought out in the evening and seats about 7 or 8 very close together. It was served by a mother & 2 sons and was really very good. Matsumoto chatted and laughed with the other customers and explained what they were saying.

This is Tuesday A.M., one week since my arrival. Last Saturday & Sunday I spent in the mountains about 70 mi from here with Brig. O'Brien's son, who drove me up in his jeep. It is in the Fujiyama region & wonderfully bold and beautiful. It was a great pleasure to get out of the city & do a little walking and climbing. We stopped at a Jap. farm house to try to get information of the way up the mountain but did not have great success. However I think the people were friendly & interested. They waved to us from below as we toiled up the steep shoulder of the mountain overlooking their farm & we waved back. We came back the same way & had more talk with them by signs. The women were busy peeling bamboo shoots.

Then we went for a swim in the lake at Hakone, which is one of the most beautiful places imaginable, and put up at a little Japanese inn overlooking it. It was miraculously clean and surrounded by a lovely garden. When we came to the door two women in kimonos greeted us, side by side, at the head of the steps. We took off our shoes, as is the universal & admirable custom, and were shown to our rooms in sandals. At the threshold of the rooms we left the sandals as one should only walk on the immaculate straw matting in bare feet. The room had moveable screens for walls on the side opening into the next room. These were ornamented paper or cloth, opaque but reaching to the ceiling. The door was a sliding screen of translucent paper, as was the outer wall opening on a long gallery. The fourth wall had a niche for a kakemono and cupboards next to it with sliding doors. There was no furniture in the room but a low central table, square, of teak, and a little mirror self-supported with two drawers, one on each side, such as might be on a dressing table. This room is bedroom, dining room and living room, according to universal custom.

We were each brought a kimono and shed our clothes. It was warm enough so that we sat on the gallery (there were straw chairs here) in the breeze off the lake with great satisfaction.

Then we went down to the bath. This is a deep well, full of excruciatingly hot water, big enough for two people to sit together immersed up to the neck. First, in the anteroom you shed your kimono & sandals. Then next the bath, you sit on a low stool and soap yourself over scrupulously with water in a wooden tub dipped from the bath. You must not get any soap or dirty water in the main bath. When you are quite clean & washed free of soap, you enter the bath. This was a matter of great agony for me. The girl, nothing abashed by our nudity, came to supervise. When I got out I was near fainting but, after walking back to our room, I found a very pleasant relaxed sensation and was in a good mood for our supper which we had, kneeling at the square table. There were several courses and it was all very good. There was not much privacy and every remark of our neighbors on the other side of the screen came to us, though of course we could not understand the Japanese. After supper was cleared away the beds were brought out. These are simply mattresses laid on the floor with handsome figured comforters to go over you. I slept well.

Next day we drove home via Atami on the sea, where the shore is very precipitous. We had a chance to see the fishing boats and went swimming along with many Japs.

That evening I had dinner with Bunker, who told me I had been invited by the Marquis of Matsudaira, the Emperor's master of ceremonies, to dinner. That will be very interesting.

Matsumoto wants to take me up to the country to have tea with the Prince Chichibu, the Emperor's brother, if I can get hold of a car. He of course has none.

No more now Yr devoted Farmy

July 5, 1950 (postmarked July 11)   *Art and Science*
                                                        JW in Tokyo to Milton

Dear Anne & Jeffy, This letter will be mailed at the same time I suppose as my last letter, for the post office is closed. I have had several adventures since I last wrote you. Young Mr. [Kyoshi] Kurahashi came to lunch with me yesterday. He is a charming boy of 28 , who is a biochemist but is also much interested in art & whose brother is now on his way home from the U.S. (Univ of Washington) where he has been studying drama.

We went to a very Japanese restaurant, quite small but where the food was delicious. The "tables," 8 inches from the ground, were in little booths or rooms with immaculate straw matting on them. There are no chairs; you sit on the floor and before entering you must take off your shoes. A girl in kimono & obi served us & Kurahashi ordered a delicious meal in this order: raw fish with sauce and condiments; a plate of lobsters covered with batter & fried in deep fat, together with beautifully cooked seaweed & something like squash or eggplants all with a special sauce; a bowl of rice; fish soup, the broth having a smoky taste & very delicious. Then there was green tea & pickles. It was much more civilized than most of our meals. Beforehand we were given steaming hot cloths to wipe our hands and faces. The chopsticks were not separated completely and our first act was to split them apart. The whole meal took some time.

Afterwards we talked some time & then we walked out & I bought some fine Japanese watercolor paper — much better than this [he's writing on large pieces of onion-skin] on which the paint runs as you will see from the mark below [a green splotch]. Then we took the subway to the National Museum at Ueno Park, where we had only time to look at the incomparable bronzes and the old costumes before closing time. Then we went to pay a call on the director, Dr. Harada who had previously taken me through the place. Afterwards we stopped for beer & fried rice and so came home to the hotel where Kurahashi left me.

The day was July 4 and in the evening I went up to look at the doings and dancing, rather crude, of my countrymen on the roof of this boisterous hotel full of officers and refugees. I enjoyed the night air until 10 & then turned in. I hope to transfer to somewhat better quarters under the assimilated title of Colonal — everyone must have a title here.

This morning I had a most difficult time. I took a taxi out to the folk museum, presided over by one Yamaji, to whom I had a letter from Langdon Warner. It was a long way off, in a very obscure place and Yamaji was away in Kyoto. They had some lovely things — chiefly ceramics, which took the very heart out of you for subtlety and beauty of color and design, and were almost equalled by the textiles. The kimonos were of course not so grand as the imperial ones at the National Museum, for they were everyday ones made of prints rather than brocades, but they were exquisite. Of course even to enter the museum I had to take off my shoes for straw sandals. But my troubles began when it was time to go home. I had no way of getting a taxi & seemed to be in the most deserted and inaccessible region conceivable. Finally by sign language I made my desires known and was taken to a house across the street belonging to the museum where I managed to call W. [?] Tagami who has been arranging my schedule. He sent up a cab which arrived in jig time to get me back to the hotel for lunch before the big meeting of which I will tell you. The distance was miles & miles.

I was to be called for by arrangement of Dr. Kamayama, by the Secretary of the J.S.C. (Japanese Science Council) and taken to their building. The Secretary & his secretary, a girl, called in a limousine with chauffeur at 1:45 and I was driven to the Science building. There I was met by the president, Dr. Kamayama, and about a dozen leading scientists of the Tokyo area in physics, biology and biochemistry. Brig. Gen. O'Brien, representing SCAP, was also there. It was very formal. Each scientist had his name printed on a card pinned to his lapel. They were sitting about a line of round tables. I was introduced all round. Then Dr. K. made a welcoming speech, to which I replied, and after that Brig. O'Brien. I don't know how much was understood. After that I was asked to say something about my scientific work, and then each scientist was asked to tell of his work very briefly.

It was certainly remarkable to see how many of us had interests and friends in common. Some had read my papers & I was well aware of the work of one of them, Dr. [Ichiro] Mizushima, who had done some famous experiments on dielectric constants. Green tea was brought in cups without handles, then fruit, then tea with lemon & sugar in cups with handles, and cakes. The most benign and courteous figure imaginable was old Dr. Hayashi, retired, with tremendous mustachios like a mandarin. Every one was delightful — each rather nervous as he said his piece. It was agreed that if my masters in the State Department accede, I should spend my time in lectures and visits at the various Japanese universities. A program for visits to the various labs in Tokyo to occupy the next week was worked out & then the plan is for me to make a tour of the country, beginning in Hokkaido & ending in Kyushu. After that a more protracted set of visits beginning in the autumn when the universities are in official season. It will be very interesting & O'Brien is to begin work on the arrangements today. He is a remarkably winning & astute man & I understand why he has such a high place at such an early age. I understand he is under consideration for a number of higher posts, among them Australian representative in U.N. So I hope he can work out my arrangements but it remains to be seen. The Japanese are anxious for it & only bureaucracy in Washington stands in the way.

Last night Dr. Kamayama & his wife took me out to dinner at a very nice restaurant. They appeared in full Japanese costume & I was humiliated that they were, as always the case, treated so rudely at the hotel desk. He wore a black ribbed silk kimono and she a violet one with a very fine pattern and the usual obi (belt with a kind of cushion like a bow behind.) It was the biggest Japanese meal I have ever had so far and lasted nearly two hours. I can't begin to tell you of all the different things we had including mushroom soup in a teapot, trout, lobsters, raw fish, tofu, sweets etc. etc. Everything is served in the most exquisite way, often in lacquered vessels, as you sit kneeling by the low table. I must mention, however, one of the best items, which was sea cucumber — something like salted sea urchins' eggs. Oriental food is really incomparable for variety, subtlety and contrast.

Friday P.M. — I have just got back from a wonderful trip with Herrington, who is in charge of the fisheries rehabilitation program here under SCAP. He once occupied space in our laboratory, years ago. We drove in his car to a most out-of-the-way region on the outside (Pacific side) of the Chiba Penninsula, which forms the northern side of Tokyo Bay.

Henceforth my address:
Scientific & Technical Division E.S.S.
G.H.Q. S.C.A.P.
A.P.O. 500, San Francisco

July 11, 1950   *Fisheries at Chiba*
                                      JW in Tokyo to Milton

Dear Anne & Jeff, I have a letter half finished in my new office headquarters in the Empire Building, Brig. O'Brien's place, but I find the whole shooting match is closed & so I will spend the rest of this intolerably hot afternoon — thermometer in the 90s, nearly 100% humidity — finishing it on a different sheet of paper.

I believe I was just about to tell you of my 2-day trip with Herrington of the fisheries section to the coast on the outside of the Chiba Penninsula, about 90 miles from here. He and his assistant, a Nisei interpreter, called to pick me up about 9:15 A.M. & we were soon wheeling out through weary waste of suburbs to the N.W. of Tokyo, crossing several rivers one after another which flow out into the great steaming expanse of Tokyo Bay. As we skirted the shore we could see the square sails of the fishing fleet — perhaps 50 vessels — far against the skyline, some dark in shadow, some white in the sun. For a mile or more, I fancy a good deal more, offshore the water is so shallow when the sea is in at high tide that a man can wade anywhere. And there were lots of clam diggers & gatherers of seaweed to be seen. Farther out still were the stakes and twine of fish weirs. After an hour or more of driving we began to drop the city and next we found ourselves in Chiba. After that we turned east to cross the mountainous peninsula.

We had left the great plain with its sluggish rivers and we soon found ourselves in the heart of the countryside, quite thickly inhabited but very isolated and rural and I should suppose still characteristic of medieval Japan. Wherever there was a chance for them we saw rice paddies, ditched and irrigated, some in the valleys, some on the terraced sides of the hills. Always there were peasants, men & women wading in the mud tending them, their legs bare with Japanese clothes and the huge umbrella-like hats you have so often seen in pictures, some concave upwards, some concave downwards. The sun was blinding and it was very steamy in the shut-in valleys. The houses with their thatched or tiled roofs, very lofty and hive-like, were in groups shaded by thickets of trees and surrounded often by clipped hedges with inviting entrance ways. Every place beyond the meanest has a cool shady garden with stones and flowers & often a pool. Often we would pass a shrine or a temple in the cool dark shade of its big trees. Each group of houses seemed to be a little island universe of its own.

Soon the country became very precipitous and the winding road took us through many tunnels bored through the limestone hills. At the divide we had long view out over the narrow valleys, each with its cultivated fields and nodding hats. The road skirted the hillside where the ground fell away so fast that it was subject to many washouts in the rainy season, which is just now past. At one place we stopped to watch two women husking their oats by pounding it with great mallets which they swung alternately in rhythm in tall wooden tubs. There were hand operated winnowing machines and much of the grain was spread out on straw mats to dry. The thing that impressed me most was the extreme localness of this medieval life. All that I had read in Genji about journeys through the countryside came back to me. And so we wound on and on as it seemed to grow hotter and hotter. Many of the men wore only loin cloths.

At last ahead of us we could see the unruffled water of the Pacific and we soon found ourselves at a little harbor in a bold coast. It was filled with odd-shaped medieval-looking boats and little fish were out drying in the sun on screens. We did not stop more than a few minutes but hurried on in order for Herrington to be on hand for a meeting with the representatives of the various groups of local fishermen. We passed through many tunnels and went by one huge and very beautiful wooden temple which I regret to say we did not have time to stop at. At last, as we followed up the coast northward, the hills began to flatten and beaches to replace rocks. At one beach we stopped to eat our sandwiches. After that we were soon in the flat country where there is a superb unbroken beach called the 99 mile beach — lined with fishing boats and little villages and a sea of rice paddies and tilled fields behind. The farms stand out like wooded islands on the fields. Just back of the beach is a slight rise suggesting dunes. The road was very winding and hard to follow and in one place we lost it.

At last we came to our destination where we were guided to the local inn — each town has one. We were greeted as usual by the girls and shed our shoes at the threshold. It was a great occasion for the governor of the province was there, as well as 20 - 30 representatives of the fishermen from along the coast, to discuss the question of shrinking supply of sardines as well as problems arising from some gunnery practice along the coast which had interfered with the operation of certain boats.

We all sat on the floor in a big room downstairs. Tea was served and the discussion went on and on and on, each English statement by Herrington seeming to be expanded into an oration by the interpreter. They were fine looking men on the whole, hard and brown beyond the usual brown of a Japanese. When at last it was over, we had the usual Japanese bath, put on yukatas (a kind of kimono) and were ready for the banquet which was given for us by the fishermen. The governor meantime, a thin inscrutable man, had left. The eating and drinking of beer & sake lasted almost two hours. Herrington sat at the head of the table, I on his right, the assistant on his left & the interpreter next me. There was much hilariousness & all the dead seriousness of the discussion was gone. The girls in their kimonos, according to custom, came and kneeled close to us and filled our glasses as we ate. Sometimes they would take us by the hand or the arm. There were all sorts of different fish dishes, both raw and cooked. At the end of the meal, one of the old men, a mayor of a near-by village, got up and did a kind of rowing dance as the others sang and clapped. Then I was made to get up and dance American fashion with one of the girls. After it was all over we went to a room upstairs, the four of us, where tea was brought us. We could hear the rote of the sea on the beach 500 yards or so away and the screens were pulled aside so that the cool breezes blew through the room.

H. & I decided to go for a night swim. One of the girls was delighted to walk down with us & she led us through the tiny passages of the village where we could see the people moving and sitting in their houses. At last we came out on the beach where we could see the great looming forms of the boats hauled up on the beach. They looked like battleships, though actually I suppose only about 40 feet long. It was a very dark night but breaking waves stood out in white rows against the blackness coming up against the boats. We gave our gowns and shoes to the girl to hold and ran down the flat beach. The water is about 78 so it did not take much courage. When we came out dripping our towels were held up for us & then our yukatas & we walked home & had a hot bath to wash the salt from us before lying down on our mats. We were each given a separate room and when we had lain down a great mosquito netting pie [sic] was spread over us. I slept fairly well until 6 when I arose to be ready for the fishing operations which we wanted to see & of which I will tell you later. But now I must go out to dinner with Brig. O'Brien.

Sunday A.M.: The boats were starting to set out about 7. We shaved, had the usual bath and were served a colossal breakfast of rice, fried seaweed, smoked baby squid, tea (of course), rice, etc. When one of us asked for an egg, a dozen were brought. I was impatient to be off and glad enough to get into the car & drive to the next village where the boat we were to go with was beached. It was a wonderful sight — a magnificent beach stretching in both directions as far as the eye could follow, very flat with the Pacific swells rolling in and breaking in series. The whole place was a hive of activity.

Each boat had its allotted stretch of beach, about 300, perhaps 500 yds long. The technique was to take a long line of seine, about 1/2 mile long, and set it in a great arc or scallop off the beach. Two ropes, one at each end, led back to the beach at the extreme ends of the range. When the net had hung in place for a time, it was hauled in, the women, say 30 of them, tailing in to one line, the men in like number to the other. Already some boats were setting and, in some cases, the nets were being hauled. It is an odd way of fishing, called beach seining, and I have seen it practised on a much smaller scale at Rio Hato in the Gulf of Panama from dugouts. The boats are very very large and heavy, unpainted, in large part pegged together, & of an immemorial pattern, [drawing]. Some, including ours, had a kind of outboard motor but others were handled entirely by sculls and poles. No sails are used for the brief operation. Each boat is about 40 feet long and must weigh many tons. They are hauled right up on the beach by sheer manpower, without benefit of tackle or windlass, between sets. All the men and women belonging to each boat are summoned when a set is to be made by squeals made with horns and by beating sticks of wood together in a kind of control tower. The signal for our people was given as we walked down the beach.

Men & women came running, the women, many either pregnant or carrying their babies on their backs. The children came too. Big greased skids were placed in a line ahead of the boat. A beam (or pole) was held across the counter, in the crack between it and the rudder, and this served directly for pushing and also a line attached to each end was used for hauling [drawing]. Some men stood on each side & tried to get the boat rocking. At first it seemed impossible that she could be moved at all but at last she began to swing back and forth a little to the shouts of Ya Sa — Ya Sa — and soon, to my amazement, she began to move down the beach. It was a wonderful sight as she moved out into the surf under the efforts of all these men and women. Then it was too hard to get the skids under the keel and keep them there until the weight came to bear on them, for the waves would wash them aside. We pushed right out into the water and then the few who actually handled the boat jumped aboard, we among them. Men with poles at the bow kept her heading right and also shoved. After a few heavy pitches were were out through the surf and soon the crew were frantically paying out the net. Before you could say Jack Robinson the setting was over and we were back off the beach again, ready to be hauled out. Some of the boys jumped overboard with lines, the men & women on the beach all reassembled, and the earlier process of launching was reversed.

But the work of hauling in the heavy seine is no less than that of setting up the boat. It is done with a great deal of chanting and shouting. Each man or woman has a line with a block of wood on it and a bight and he siezes onto the main line with this and walks in with it [drawing]. The men were many of them quite naked & the women bare to the waist but often, as I say, with their babies strapped to their backs. Some would stop to suckle the babies during the operation. There was great excitement as the net came in. All hands stood by to shake it down & work the fish into the bunt. It was a poor catch on the whole. The fish were bailed out of the net in big baskets and carried up to the waiting ox carts on the beach. Everyone seemed very happy & I never realized with greater force the beauty of human labor — The people were all so strong, so healthy, so beautiful & so happy. I had a swim & then we went back to the captain's house where we washed and were given another feast before we drove home.

When I got back I paid a call on Brig. O'Brien & found the arrangements about my stay in Japan had all been completed in his office. I shall be in Tokyo about 10 days more, & then start for Hokkaido etc.

Yesterday morning I had the first meeting at the University — a kind of round table conference. The dinner in the evening with Brig. O'Brien was most interesting but I will tell you of it later for Mr. Kurahashi is coming to take me to Kamakura for the day.

Lots & lots of love, Farmy

July 11, 1950 (postmarked July 18)   *Picnic at Kamakura*
JW in Tokyo to Marblehead

Dear Anne & Jeff, I posted you a letter yesterday, giving my address. I am sending all my letters to Marblehead because I am sure they will reach you there. This is the 4th letter I have written from Japan. Will you please let me know whether the other three have reached you. [Gives address.] So far I have had no word from home but it is no wonder considering the confusion of the Korean War.

These are the events since I last wrote you. On Sat A.M. I went to a meeting of various scientists in the Tokyo area at Dr. Hayashi's laboratory at the Imp. University. He is a great figure, though emeritus, most dignified and with big mustaches as I think I wrote you. He presented me with a Chinese fan. It is quite common to give a fan here. Then we had a round table conference in which the work of the members of Dr. Kodama's dept of Biochem. was outlined. Dr. [Yoshiaki] Miura had lunch with me in a nice little Jap restaurant near the Ginza afterwards.

In the evening I went out to Brig. O'Brien's house with the wonderful garden. I wrote you of it before. We all sat out in the garden and had mint juleps as dusk fell. The servants brought out joss sticks or coils which they distributed about the grass to keep away mosquitos. These were present: a couple from the Canadian legation, the wife of an English businessman, an Australian couple, he a member of the U.N. commission in Korea who had that day flown back from there and was most interesting; the O'Bs & myself. [8 people.] I gather the situation is very serious in Korea and it is a toss-up whether or not we lose the whole peninsula. The armored trucks of the N Koreans are very strong and the weather is so bad — rainy season just beginning — that our planes can do little. Newspaper reports gloss over all reverses as usual & one cannot go by what one reads in the Stars & Stripes here. The Australian was to fly back yesterday A.M. I got home at midnight — very hot — & slept as usual bare naked with no sheet until morning.

Next day, being Sunday, was free & I went down to an ancient coastal city called Kamakura about an hour from here by train with young Kurahashi. We started at 10:30 and, as Kamakura has the most famous of the nearby beaches, the station was swarming with people. I took your little weekend case, which has proved most useful, with my bathing suit in it. Most of the trip was dull, taking us through Yokahama which is about like Jersey City. It was a great relief to get at last to Kamakura. It was once the capital of Japan (about 1200 AD). It lies back of the beach, where the sea takes a great bite out of the land, and is completely surrounded by bold limestone hills, through which the train enters by tunnel. Although it is now something of a resort, it retains much of its ancient character. In old days there were the following classes: Court nobles, soldiers or knights (Samurai), farmers, craftsmen, merchants, in that order of rank. Part of the city was prohibited to all but the Samurai and nobles. Of the rest, certain streets were devoted to certain workers, eg. stone cutters, fishermen, wood workers. Much of this still survives. Kurahashi's uncle by marriage lives there & we went at once to his house.

He is quite a character — I gather of old Samurai stock & a member of the Heiki clan as Kurahashi is of the Genji clan. He speaks good English & better German & recited part of Childe Harold to me. He lost everything — home, wife & daughter in the bombing of Tokyo and has now, Jap. fashion, adopted a rather pretty girl of 25 as his daughter along with her mother & father. I suppose that means she is, in effect, his wife somewhat as in the Tale of Genji with the adopted girls. He now owns or at least runs a boatyard in Tokyo where they build yachts. But he is learned in the art, history & customs of Japan.

We went down to the beach to swim — Kurahashi, the uncle, the girl and a friend & I, equipped with a beach umbrella, a picnic lunch and in our bathing suits. It was a beautiful beach & there was a high on-shore wind which made a fine surf. The water was about 78 I should think & the beach was black or rather brown with people for they were of course all Japanese & wore rather brief bathing suits — many of the boys only a loin cloth. It was interesting to see all the different types — on the whole very good looking and well behaved. The beach must be about a mile long and there were perhaps 20,000 people there. After a swim, we had our lunch which consisted of balls of rice wrapped in seaweed and fried fish. Then we walked along the beach & watched some games & some Japanese wrestling matches. It was wonderful to see a tiny little fellow, as strong as an ant, tip over his much bigger antagonists. In the middle of the afternoon we went back to the house where the girl's mother had the usual hot bath ready for us in the wooden tub, bathed & dressed.

Then we walked through to the train where we stopped at the shops of various artisans: a joiner who had the most exquisite set of Japanese planes which one pulls towards one instead of pushing; a saw sharpener (& perhaps maker) who was a fat elderly man working away in a loin cloth (Jap. saws are like big serrated knives and are pulled rather than pushed, like the plane); a maker of scrolls (for writing notes) and also of screens; a dyer; a dealer in Buddhist temple furniture. It is a charming city and these simple people were all most friendly & courteous. And then we took a crowded bus — the most crowded I have ever been in— and rode about 2 miles to a shop where we got off to see a Zen Buddhist temple of the old Kamakura era.

You must not think of it as a single building, or even a group of buildings, but as a kind of peaceful garden or park. We ascended a long flight of much worn limestone steps in the deep shade of the great cedar trees and came to a tremendous gateway [drawing] very simply built of wood, without a single nail, and with thatched or straw roof. There was some carving but the beauty and majesty of it all came from the proportions and setting. Beyond it we came into a great open space shaded by cedars and closed in by the towering and diversely wooded walls of the steep limestone hills, with naked cliffs from which sprang many ferns here & there. There were other buildings for eating and sleeping and paths and stairways leading off in different directions. It was all a garden of the most sophisticated sort, originated I believe by a Chinese gardener in the 12th or 13th century and nursed by the priests ever since. As we walked on we passed a pool with Japanese maples and oaks overhanging it and goldfish rising in the amber colored water. The only bright color was the blue of the mountain hydrangeas. Then we went farther up the valley, following a much worn path and up more steps until we came to another set of buildings. There the uncle walked up to a paper covered wall. A slide was opened and a priest came out. He asked us in while he went to get the key to a kind of sanctuary building nearby where there was a carved Buddha. Later we went up another flight of steps to a kind of bell tower where there was the most enormous bronze bell, rung by a hanging log.

July 13, 1950   *Dinner with Geishas*
                                        JW in Tokyo to Marblehead

Dear Anne & Jeff, I am always in the prodicament of having a half-finished letter in some other place just when I have a good chance to write you. So it is now at 6:30 on Thursday July 13. I daresay there is more confusion at home over the Korean War than there is right here in Tokyo, within a few hours (3 or 4) by air of the front. I have a chat about it every morning with John O'Brien who is commander in chief of the Commonwealth forces in Japan. He takes a very sensible view, having fought on most fronts of the last war: we can't do much until we have a far greater weight of air power & good forces are built up; and the best we can hope for in the immediate future is the stabilization of a line somewhere way down the peninsula; we are bound to win in the end; the notion of getting other troops into a field (i.e. other than our own) is not wise except perhaps as a token, for they are not needed and will only complicate the command situation.

But I find myself asking What if we do win? Unless we go beyond the 38th Parallel or establish a semi-permanent occupation the whole thing may happen over again & there is no real assurance of anything. But if we do, we provide the basis for a strong propaganda from the

Soviets & Chinese communists that we are playing an unpleasant role and that we have at last shown our hand. It links us very strongly with the Chinese Nationalists & the French in Indochina & the Dutch in Java & the British in the Malay and may turn the whole of the Orient against us. I think the most unwise thing we could do would be to use the bomb.

But so much for all this. Let me tell you of my doings. I believe I left off with an account of the Zen Buddhist temple at Kamakura. I will say no more of that. After seeing it, we returned to the main part of the town & saw several other temple objects. One huge & to me rather unattractive gold Buddha, about 30 feet high, and one superb bronze outdoor Buddha from about 1200. The latter was a sitting figure perhaps 35 - 40 ft high, very serene and very beautiful. It has weathered to a most wonderful green color and must be much more beautiful than when it was new. It is a triumph of technology and was cast in innumerable small pieces which were later secured together with molten bronze. It is of course hollow and you can go inside and climb about on a staging. Afterwards we went back to the Uncle's house where we were given a supper prepared (but not shared) by the women & so home to the hotel where I arrived about 11 P.M.

Next day was a busy one. I gave a lecture in the A.M. on the physical chem of hemoglobin, then listened to a short talk in reply by a Japanese worker. We had a very fine discussion, one of the keenest I have taken part in, largely due to Prof Mizushima. Then I ate a picnic lunch with Prof Kodama & some of his assistants, was taken over their laboratory, and finally driven down to the Ministry of Education for a general discussion of my stay in Japan.

But the evening was the more interesting part of the day & interesting it was indeed. I had been asked to dine with the Marquis of Matsudaira, the Emperor's Master of Ceremonies. This was not to be in his house, as I discovered, for such affairs are not given at home. Precisely at 7 I was called for by Kurada & we drove to the blank enigmatic wooden front of a low house in a very Japanese lane. There Kurada and I entered, removed our shoes and were shown by the waiting girls into an exquisite room where we were received by M[atsudira], who would be recognized for a great aristocrat in any company. The walls were screens. There was an alcove with flowers and kakemono. In the centre was the usual low table & 3 cushions on the mat or Tatami, one for each of us three. I was invited to take a bath and shed my European clothes, which I gladly did. When I reappeared in a blue cotton yukata I found the others similarly dressed and the table laid out with the first course. About 4 Geisha girls sat by and served us and made conversation which of course was lost on me. We began with smoked abalone and Japanese beer but soon passed on to sake wh. we drank from tiny cups. I was shown the manner of drinking healths and passing the cup for a third person to pour. Since women do not eat with men, according to the customs of old Japan as I understand them, the geishas take their places as professional entertainers. But I do not think of them as prostitutes. I cannot tell you all the courses we enjoyed but the eating went on intermittently for about 2 hours to the sound of dripping water in the garden on which one side of our room opened. We were aware of no other guests in the house though I believe there was one other group.

Do not think we overate by any means, simply because we ate so many things and so long. It was very pleasant and informal and the time passed quickly. A new set of geishas came in after a time, one of whom played a Japanese three-stringed lute and sang. I expressed an interest in the tea ceremony and this was staged for us but not, of course, with the true formality & decorum. M[atsudira] offered to give me some letters that would introduce me to some Jap. householders as I journey and one in particular to his brother-in-law, the Marquis of Tokugawa, descendant of the Shoguns, when I go to Nikko this weekend as I mean to do, taking young Kurahashi as my guest & guide. (I have told him he must be prepared to walk.) At 10:30 precisely I took my leave with Kurada who escorted me home. The geishas helped us with our clothes and marvelled at my nylon shirts and zippers, bowed low to the ground as we made our exit & clustered round the car as we drove off. It was one of the great times of my memory.

The following day I spent with Mizushima, who is the Professor of physical chemistry at Tokyo Univ. & also has a group of people at the Institute of Science & Technology at Komba of which he was, until recently, director. We spent the morning at the university where we had a kind of symposium and then a visit to the labs, and the afternoon similarly at the Inst. He drove back with me afterwards & we dined together on tempura, a special kind of giant shrimp fried in batter. Then we strolled down the Ginza, had some Jap cakes & tea and so parted & I went home. Miz. is a most ingenuous man with about 30 assistant & graduate students, and nearly all his very beautiful optical and physical equipment has been made in his lab. He has a very skillful mechanic who gets $1.00 a day. He has worked along some of the same lines I have and has been applying some of my results on dielectric constants to his own work. We shall see more of one another. [Prof. Mizushima once came to lunch in Milton and took ACW to Kamakura in his car on her visit to Japan in May, 1970. A Roman Catholic, he'd once had an audience with the Pope.]

The next day, Wednesday, I spent the A.M. with Prof Sakamoto of physiology & the P.M. with Prof Okada, who used to be the dean of the faculty and is a most delightful simple man with a wonderful sense of humor. He is a zoologist who has been much in France. In the evening I went to supper with Dr. Miura, who is a young biochemist. He lives in a tiny little house in the garden of his father's house which, except for a few rooms, has been comandeered by SCAP as living quarters for a colonel. The old father is 86, bent almost double, but a master of German and English and I believe French, who was physician to the last emperor and was the leading neurologist of Japan, I gather. He was educated in Germany. He came in after supper to see me and told me of knowing H[arvey] Cushing [a noted Boston M.D.], old Dr. Welsh & others on his visit to U.S.A. He also told me of his early memories which go back to the pre-Meiji era when Japan was a locked country & the Shogun still ruled. As a boy he travelled all the way from Sendai [north of Tokyo on the Pacific] to Tokyo in a jinricksha which took two weeks. How I wish I could have seen the old Japan before this horrible westernization.

I was also shown some family photographs of his father-in-law [the Count Hirata] taken in Paris in the days of Napoleon III along with other members of the Japanese embassy, all with swords in Samurai dress. The other son and his wife & son (19) as well as a cousin, who is professor of Physical Chem at Osaka & whom I shall see later in my travels, also came in after supper. The cousin is a great friend of Mizushima. Supper was a very simple meal cooked & shared by Miura's wife. The two young daughters (3 & 5) were there also.

This brings me to today which was a free day as far as science goes. I went to the Empire Building after breakfast to arrange about the journey to come & then picked up Miura, his wife and the 19-year old nephew on my way to pay a 3rd visit to the Nat'l Museum & to old Dr. Harada. The pictures had largely been changed since my last visit & are quite overwhelming. There were some very beautiful kakemonos & makimonos from the Kamakura period and some big screens from the end of the 15th to end of 16th centuries. Afterwards I took the Miuras out to lunch.

In the morning I had received a note from Kurada at the palace saying that Matsudaira had arranged for me to go to a real, serious tea ceremony at the Byutsu Club where I once went to see Baron Dan. We had arranged that Kurada would call for me at 3 & I was ready. It was quite an experience: something like Holy Communion. The implements are all very beautiful & very old — 300 to 500 years and highly precious. I had the ceremony 3 times, the first two times in a big room & the third in a real tea room. The room always has a very exquisite but simple arragement of flowers in 1 vase and some particularly precious kakemono. You all kneel in a circle round the room while the powdered green tea is infused with water heated over a little charcoal brazier in a special silver pot. It is measured out in a bamboo spoon from a very precious lacquered or porcelain box into an earthenware bowl, somewhat irregular; water is added & the mixture beaten with a whisk. The result is a rather bitter greenish froth of suspended tea powder. It is not at all like ordinary tea. While all this is going on, you must make polite conversation and admire all the equipment, the flowers and the picture. Before you take the tea, a basket of sweets is passed to which you help yourself with chopsticks. Then the bowl of tea is placed before you and you take it in both hands, turn it until the somewhat irregular rim is in exactly the right position (you may feel the rim while doing this) and then drink the tea in exactly three draughts. Then you put the bowl down, give it a quarter turn and wipe the rim with a piece of rice paper which you then drop into the sleeve of yr kimono. Everyone watches you (though very politely) while you do this. There is also another procedure, involving somewhat thicker pasty tea, in which the bowl is passed from person to person, the edge being wiped between times. I took part in this as well. After it was over we went upstairs and had some sake, sweets & savories with some of the others. One of the ladies presented me with a fan describing the rules of the ceremony. Farmy

---

July 18, 1950 (postmarked July 24) *Turtles and Temples*
JW in Tokyo to Marblehead

Dear Anne & Jeff, I hope I am not boring you with all these minute accounts of my doings here. Writing to you both is next best to seeing you. I am sending all the letters to ACW c/o Walcotts as the most certain address. I have heard nothing from home so far and am anxious to do so, naturally.

Last Friday I was called for by Dr. Muraji and got a car & chauffeur from SCAP to drive us down to a marine biological station at Misake, which is a miniature counterpart of our Woods Hole below Kamakura at the end of the small Izu penninsula that forms the S.W. side of Tokyo Bay. It is close to the place where Com[modore Matthew Galbraith] Perry made his famous landing nearly 100 years ago and on the way home we drove through there. The greater part of the drive was very dull, taking us through the great industrial area between here & Yokahama & beyond. Then we went past the great naval base at Yokosuka and into rather mild farming country. Just before reaching Misake we stopped to pick up Dr. Dan & his wife who work at Misake. He is the son of the old Baron Dan who was assassinated just before the war and is an attractive good looking man who studied at the Univ of Penn for a number of years before the war. I suppose he is about 40 years old or a little more. His wife is an American, also a biologist, and a most agreeable woman. They have 5 children. We stopped at their pleasant house in the depths of the country with its gate, garden and great thatched roof of pyramidal form. The roof is the chief external architectural feature of a Japanese house. Inside the house was basically Japanese but it had European chairs & tables in it. Mrs D. has been 13 years in Japan & seems to speak quite well.

Misake proved to be a lovely little place with a great inlet where there was a fishing village. The lab & aquarium were somewhat run down but interesting. We saw some huge sea turtles in the aquarium and fed them conchs on the end of a bamboo pole. These they crushed with a loud noise between their beak-like jaws and spat out the shell. The turtle is an emblem of drunkenness in Japan and it is said that the fishermen often ply them with sake until they are intoxicated and then let them go. We had lunch at the lab and then some demonstrations and quite a long discussion until I left at 3 or 3:30. I got home about 6:30 and had my only solitary dinner since I have been here & the first one to eat in the hotel.

Dr Muraji was extrememly interesting in his description of the Hiroshima bomb. He & Nishina, the famous Jap physicist who had the Jap cyclotron that was later destroyed & whom I am going to see this P.M., were summoned at once to the scene & were the first scientists to see the destruction. The first news of the falling of the atom bomb came from the U.S. short-wave radio & was picked up at once by the war office. M. said the disappearance of secondary radiation was vastly more rapid than had been anticipated, though if the bomb had been dropped in water as at Bikini the situation would have been quite different. He said there was great immediate destruction & that a great many deaths occurred 3 weeks afterwards, partly due to a destruction of red cells. In his mind there was no question that the horrors of the atomic bomb have not been exaggerated. I hope later to go to Hiroshima myself.

On Saturday Kurahashi called for me at the hotel & we took the 3rd class train up to Nikko, which was nearly a 4 hour journey. Most of it was through the great plain of Tokyo with its interminable rice paddies & gardens and clusters of houses enveloped in trees. Here & there a larger roof than usual told us of a shrine or temple. (Shrines are part of Shinto [ancestor worship]; temples belong to Buddhism.) People with their great straw hats were bent double over the fields. Often they had baskets on their backs. The clustered houses and their gardens formed wooded islands in the sea of rice. But there were other crops — soy beans, vegetables, corn, potatoes as well. The train was crowded but we had seats. K had brought sandwiches and at one of the stations we got a pot of tea. [drawing] I have the earthenware pot on my bureau. The whole thing was 3 cents (10 yen). By & by we caught our first glimpse of the serrated hills on the horizon — crazy shapes, in great folds, just as in Jap pictures, and soon we were climbing up into them. The villages became more interesting, at least as a contrast.

As we approached Nikko, which is famous for its temples & shrines, sponsored by the Tokugawa family and built in the rococo style about 300 years ago, we came upon a wonderful avenue of cryptomeria trees. It was laid out 300 years ago as an approach to Nikko by a certain Daimyo (great lord) of the Matsudaira family and took 10 years to build. It is many miles long. The trees are very large and beautiful, some 200 ft tall or more, and are a kind of cedar related to our California redwood. They are planted very close and the trunks are in many cases fused. We were so fascinated by them that we decided to get out & walk — it was only 1 1/2 hours — and I was glad we did. A gurgling brook ran down by the old road, in many places worn into a deep gully in the course of centuries and here and there ducked under the road. In other places it flowed through various farmyards and even under the outbuildings and turned many wooden water wheels which operated stone grist mills and other devices.

We stopped at several of the farms, one very prosperous one in particular. It was interesting to see the arrangement of rooms, "fire place" (a pit in the centre of the room) & sliding paper walls. At another house we watched a very skillful carpenter hewing a beam with an adze to make a partition to shut off the horse stall from the kitchen because the owner had decided it would be more hygienic so. By & by, rather hot, we reached Nikko. We were armed with letters from Prince Tokugawa, one to the temple, one to the big shrine, which is most gorgeous but not the most beautiful in Japan. Since Nikko is a memorial to Tokugawa's ancestors, the 1st or 3rd Shoguns, you may imagine that we were well received. But we went first to the hotel where they had been notified that we were coming.

There we were guided down to the Buddhist temple where we were received by a priest and taken into the inner room, or suite of rooms. The head priest is always of very high family and at times has been the emperor himself or some member of his family. The head priest was not there when we were there. We were given tea in a room overlooking an enclosed garden with a miniature artificial lake through which water was flowing. It contained a bridge & island in replica of one of the famous lakes of Japan. It was exquisitely planted and behind, as a backdrop, were the steep slopes of the mountains opposite. Peaceful indeed but the young priest said he would like to go to Tokyo — that he was weary of the continual quietness of his life. He said he hoped I would mention his name to Prince Tokugawa — in the interests of preferment I suppose.

The altars with their burning candles and lacquered reliquaries were silent as the grave. There were some magnificent screens and kakemonos of the early Tokugawa period to be seen. It was all far more remote from any breath of life than any aspect of religion in the West unless it be perhaps that of the Trappists. When we went to the shrine we found the deputy high priest waiting for us at the gate, dressed in white above and purple silk below. That shrine is the most gorgeous in Japan and is tremendous, including a score of buildings such as a stable where the dedicated horses, never driven or ridden, were lodged. It is covered with gold leaf, much carved, and also painted in bright colors.

We did not spend the night in Nikko but went up the mountain above the famous waterfall to Lake Chusenji (there is a cable car which takes you up) & made our way to a little Japanese hotel on the edge of a most beautiful lake with a volcanic peak on one side and a jagged line of more distant mountains, fold upon fold, opposite. We swam, had the usual hot bath, put on our yukatas & dined on many courses, kneeling on the floor. I much prefer the Jap. hotels to any others. Among other things, we had some pink trout.

Next day we swam and breakfasted as follows: soy bean soup, octopus paste, fried fish, eggs, rice, two kinds of seaweed & other things I have forgotten. Afterwards we took a bus to an upper lake where there are some hot sulfur springs and walked up into the heart of the mountains where we swam in a deep clear mountain lake. We saw some of the most beautiful snow white waterfalls I have ever seen — one 450 feet high. We got back to Nikko in time to have another visit to the shrine with the high priest & see the inner treasures. We met one of the cabinet ministers there, whom I did not take to, but with whom & the priest we had our pictures taken. We took the train back to Tokyo & got in by bed time.

On Monday I went out to an outlying Physical Institute for most of the day where there is quite a remarkable theoretical physicist working on many problems I have been concerned with. He has just written a book in which he showed me citations to some of my papers. After lunch I gave an informal talk. That evening I went to a garden party at Col. Schenk's house, where some Japanese people from the court as well as some university people from Stanford were present.

Tuesday I went to see the silk institute and watched the unwinding of cocoons. One fibre is about 1 mile long! Then to St Paul University with Dr. Muraji where I heard of some interesting experiments on slime molds, & so home. In the evening I went to dinner with Kurahashi's mother, brother who has just come back from U.S.A. where he studied drama, Kyoshi [Kurahashi] and a friend of the mother's. To bed at midnight.

Yesterday I went to see Nishina, whom I did not get to see earlier as planned. He is the most remarkable scientific figure in Japan — a dumpy little man with long hair, warts on his face & spectacles. He is a theoretical physicist and spent some years with [Niels] Bohr in Copenhagen. But now he is engaged in rehabiltating Jap industry by putting it in touch with science. He is president of a large company, partly commercial, partly for pure science. They have [made] much money by producing penicillin. Afterwards I had a call from young Okhi from Kyushu, whom I had corresponded with, & spent the balance of the day with Mizushima & his family, of which I will write later.

No more now. I take the train for Hokkaido tonight, a 36 hour trip to a cooler place. Love Farmy

It is nice to be associated with Jack O'Brien. No red tape. Love to the Walcotts.

July 25, 1950 (postmarked August 6)   *North with the Ainus*
JW in Hokkaido to Marblehead

Dear Anne & Jeff, I believe my last letter ended with my telling you of the fact that I spent last Thursday with Prof. Mizushima. He had told me he would take me to an interesting Japanese city house.

It turned out to be the house of his father-in-law in an outlying part of Tokyo. We took an elevated train to get there & then had something of a walk. It was a large house surrounded by a wall with a kind of garden in the front yard, very attractive with small trees, a stone lantern or two all in the Japanese style. But the house was fairly new. At the threshold, where we shed our shoes, we were greeted by his [Mizushima's] wife & two girls. I discovered we were to be given lunch there which his wife was supervising. One of the girls was about 5, the other about 10-12. The wife was very much of a home body, in her 40s, but missing a good many teeth. Japanese teeth are usually bad. We were ushered into a front parlor in European style with a fireplace & coal grate, rather ugly striped chairs, a centre table on which tea was served. The windows, which were of frosted glass to give the effect of the Jap. shoji (screens) opened on a little courtyard with bamboo & other plants growing in it. Flowers were arranged everywhere. After we had talked for a while, I was taken over the rest of the house which was Japanese. It had two floors & the main rooms at the rear and side opened on to a nice large garden. There was, as is common, a kind of passage running round this which was entirely open to the garden but could be closed by sliding screens & windows. Each room had its tokonoma or alcove & low shelf for a flower and a piece of precious porcelain or lacquer, and a low table in the middle. One room had some bookcases. Upstairs the arrangement was somewhat the same. They also showed me their storage chamber, which all well-to-do homes have (in case of fire). It was made of concrete, two stories high, and opened by iron doors like those of a safe into the main part of the house.

Mizushima & his family are Catholics and very convinced ones. We were served a very elaborate and delicious meal by the girls which their mother ate with us. Many courses including raw fish, shrimp etc. I have learned to use hashi or chopsticks fairly well now. After lunch M's sister who lives nearby came in. She has knowledge of the wood burning ceremony which is quite rare and has never been seen by most Japanese. It is much more aristocratic than the tea ceremony, as I understand it, and used to be practised by the daimyos in their palaces. A beautiful inlaid and lacquered box, about 16-18 inches sq., was brought out. When it was opened the most wonderful smell of camphor and sandalwood came from it. It was of early Tokugawa time. Various utensils were brought out, including some exquisite gold lacquered trays and a precious porcelain jar filled with fine pink ashes. There were also little tools such as a tiny silver-tipped spoon or spatula & two chopstick-like instruments for handling the coals. A glowing lump of charcoal was brought out and placed with the sticks in a crater-like hole in the ashes in the little porcelain jar. It was then all covered with a mound of ashes except for a little hole, so that the whole thing was like a small volcano. Then, with the silver chopsticks, a little mica plate about 1/2 in. square was placed over the hole and on this was laid a tiny chip of some precious wood from one or other of a number of little packages wrapped up in thin paper. When it began to smoke, the cup was held under one's nose like a tea cup, covered partially with the left hand so as to concentrate the smell. It was all quite exquisite.

I am told there used to be a game consisting of offering some combination of smells to be guessed by the "opponent." There were some 100 different smells to be recognized. I must say it was a most refined kind of game, something like wine tasting.

In the middle of the afternoon Mizushima took me off to one of the famous slum districts of Tokyo, near the Asakusa R.R. station, where we strolled about before returning to the Ginza to have some ice cream. I wanted no supper.

Next day (Friday) was my last in Tokyo. I was to leave for Hokkaido (the northern island) in the evening. I spent the morning interviewing a man from Keio University, the oldest private university in Japan, who came on behalf of the president to ask if I would give some lectures there in October when I shall be lecturing at Tokyo University according to the present schedule. I am going to give 3 sets of lectures at Tokyo. I also made arrangements for my tickets and winding up various affairs. In the late afternoon I had a farewell call from Kurahashi and then went to dinner with a man named Frew of the embassy in the Am. Club. Thence I went to my train where I shared a compartment with an interesting individual named Tindale who was also going to Hokkaido in connection with the democratization propaganda and organization being put across by SCAP. He comes from near Plymouth, Mass. The journey to Sapporo takes 36 hours & was extremely hot and dirty except for the magnificent 5 hr trip across the straits of Hokkaido.

As we approached the tip of Honshu, or rather the port at the base of the great Bay, we had a superb view of the mountains, glassy sea and towering white clouds. The whole train, after being broken up into sections, was taken onto the 3000-ton ship. The great bay is almost 40-50 miles across, with a narrow entrance made by precipitous mountains, very wild. There are only a few isolated fishing towns along the shore. You can see the towering outlines of Hokkaido long before you lose sight of Honshu and, as we entered the corresponding bay on Hokkaido, the sun was setting in the west with great effect on the mountains and sea. Tindale and I and another had a walk about Hokkaido [Hakodate] while we waited for the train to be made up. Then we went to bed and next morning when I awoke we were only two hours from Sapporo, the capital of the island.

You might describe Hokkaido as the Northwest, or even Alaska, of Japan. 80 years ago, at the time of the Meiji revolution, it had a population of only 20 - 30,000, mostly Ainus, and was an almost wholly undeveloped place. Since then there has been a great immigration from Honshu, cities and factories have been built, land has been cleared and the population has risen to several millions. The poor old Ainus have been largely crowded out. But there is a great contrast between Hokkaido and the intensively cultivated, garden-like Honshu, all on such an exquisite miniature scale like the Japanese people themselves. The country is more open and on a larger scale and there are areas of virgin forest and uncultivated land such as are to be found in old Japan. It is very beautiful in a different way, somewhat as the state of Washington is different from Vermont.

At Sapporo we were met by representatives of the Civil Affairs Division of SCAP and taken to the hotel occupied by the Americans, not so nice as the Japanese hotels but I had essentially free lodging there. At the hotel Prof Nakamura, a biochemist from the university, was awaiting me. The day being Sunday, I did not go to the university but joined Tindale in driving round the environs of the city and going to a dinner given to him by some Japanese. There are 200,000 people in Sapporo, which is a modern town on the site of an old Ainu village, and it lies on the river in a fertile plain at the edge of a range of fine mountains where there is said to be wonderful skiing all winter, which the Japanese there practise and are very good at. [It was the site of the 1972 Winter Olympics.] In winter it is very cold and the snow lies 4 feet deep, sometimes 10 ft! (so they say), about Sapporo. But in summer it is very hot though not quite as hot as Honshu and the nights are cooler. I have slept without anything on throughout my whole stay there and have only worn my little washable coat occasionally for appearance's sake.

The party was given in an inn on the outskirts of the city with the usual entertainment of geishas. There were four of us and much food of all kinds, beer and sake. In the evening I strolled about the town with Tindale and finally saw him off on his way to the opening of a Jap recreation conference at another part of the island. He invited me to join him and other members of the civil affairs group at a fair in Ashagawa towards the end of the week in a private R.R. car for U.S. officials but I decided against it in order to do better things as you will hear.

On Monday Nakamura took me to the university where I was introduced to a variety of scientific people in the office of Suganome, dean of the Fac. of Science. Before that, however, I made my official call on the commanding colonel of Civil Affairs and on the vice governor of Hokkaido, who is a remarkable little man, most friendly and most devoted to the welfare of the island. He speaks beautiful English, having been educated in U.S. & Europe & is a distinguished person with a charming wife. His house had recently burned down and he had been temporarily living with Col. Switzer. He insisted on driving Nakamura & me to the university.

I spent the rest of that day and the two following in various laboratories & institutes belonging to the university and on Tuesday delivered a lecture which I am afraid some of the audience found it hard to understand for reasons of language. But people were standing. On Monday P.M. we had a very informal beer party at the Medical Fac. (Japanese beer, which is made in Hokkaido, is delicious though an innovation.) In the evening Suganome dined with me at a very nice Jap. hotel. Tuesday before my lecture I was given a lunch at the Institute of Applied Electricity. In the evening I dined with Suganome and a man named Prof Sakamura on a perfect feast including sukiaki cooked in a charcoal brazier on the table. Sakamura sang some Noh music (which is a kind of dramatic chanting) afterwards.

On Wed P.M. I was given a formal tea party. On Thursday it was arraged that I should set off with Nakamura [the biochemist] to one of the remote parts of the island in order to have a look at the Ainus. We started at 7 and after about 2 hours on the main line train changed to a tiny branch line towards X [map]. It took about 2 hours on this train to get to Mukawa which you may find in the map. We went 3rd class — there was no other way and in any case I prefer it as you see more of the people. As usual, the train was fearfully crowded so we were taken into the mail car until seats could be found. There is much horse raising in this part of Hokkaido and the coastal region is flat with mountains in the background. It was good, as the train skirted the shore, to see the grazing horses silhouetted against the sea. By and by, at the next stop beyond Mukawa, we changed again to a still small-er line and travelled an hour or two inland up into the hills.

The average speed of train travel in Hokkaido is about 10 mph but this train must have been slower for, when it was going full speed, a man ran after it and caught up with it and jumped aboard. We came to the end of the line at a little place called Bilatori which is, in part, an Ainu town. There we had an introduction to a well-to-do Ainu who gave us some lunch to supplement the rice which Nakamura had brought and then arranged to take us up to a real Ainu village where he had an uncle and where we could spend the night. There was a daily bus leading up into the region. In the meantime we wandered about Bilatori, visited a shrine and stuck our noses into various shops.

It is good to see the life of a Japanese village. Each artisan or shop-keeper lives at the back of his place of business. We watched some blacksmiths forging an axe head. Three of them worked for an hour on one head. They were wonderfully built powerful men. One, the master, heated and held the metal while the others struck. I felt like the Pied Piper of Hamlin as I passed through the streets for I was fol-lowed everywhere by a crowd of wondering children. At last we decid-ed to start walking toward our destination and let the bus overtake us, so off we set. By and by the bus carrying the Ainu man overtook us and by evening we were at our destination. We were armed with two bottles of spirits. The houses were primitive, much in the old Japanese

style and not too dirty. In ours lived an Ainu man with his married daughter and her child. There were perhaps 30 houses in the village, arranged somewhat irregularly with well-trodden & well-swept paths leading between them. There is a town water supply consisting of a trough made of half logs, hollowed out, leading from a spring, where we washed. We were taken to one house where there was a man carving and an ancient wrinkled crone weaving string from bark with the aid of her teeth (or gums?). I kept thinking of the lines of Meg Merrilies [in Sir Walter Scott's Guy Mannering] "Twist ye, twine ye."

We walked about with our Ainu host until supper should be ready. When it was ready we were joined by a neighbor so that, altogether with the nephew from Bilatori, we were 5 as we sat cross legged on the floor. The Ainus put on their curious quilted or patchwork kimonos and our host wore a kind of crown with a carved bear, the Ainu emblem and sacred animal, at one end. [drawing] They brought out some family treasures in the form of large lacquered sake bowls and stands, which were old, for use with our gift of spirits. Various invocations and incantations were made before drinking and eating. Supper went on a long time and ended with a bowl of fresh peas still in the pods. After supper there was a little singing and then the futons (beds) were laid out & we went to sleep.

The older married Ainu women are much tatooed on the arms and about the mouth. The lips and surrounding parts are tatooed to give the impression of a mustache but the custom is now prohibited. The Ainus are a problem to the anthropologists. They have a white skin, dark eyes, are hairy like Europeans and are often supposed to belong to the Caucasian race. Previously they are known to have occupied a large part of Japan but in the course of centuries have been driven farther & farther back. Until recently they have lived almost in the manner of the Stone Age.

Next day our Ainu host took us by bus still higher up in the mountains and after a ride on a Jap lumber truck we found ourselves in another village. There we made a fairly long circuit over hill & dale and arrived by midday at another Ainu village after a swim in the river, which was delicious. In the afternoon we walked up into the hills in quest of some Ainu charcoal burners but found only their kilns. That evening we dined by invitation (ie Nakamura & I) with a Japanese lumber man who had a nice home near the village where our host lived. We had a hot bath, were supplied with yukatas and passed a pleasant evening until we were taken back to Bilatori by our host's truck. We spent the night at a little inn at Bilatori & set out at 5 A.M. for Urakawa, still further down the penninsula, which I was resolved to cross on foot. Nakamura had to go back but said he knew of a boy from from Urakawa who he thought would accompany me and was a strong fellow being a member of the Sapporo university rugby football team. There was a horse fair at Urakawa but we went direct to the subprefectural office to enquire about the possibility of crossing the mountains, which seemed to be very questionable. Meanwhile a messenger was sent for the boy. We were given some contour maps but no one seemed to know anything about crossing the mountains and we were sent on to the headquarters of the forestry department, leaving word for the boy to follow. The forestry people seemed to be as ignorant as anyone else but finally it was agreed that there was a way, though a bad one, which might be found.

At this point the boy came in, quite hot from hurrying after us. He was a fine looking fellow of 22 with a wonderful physique, about 2 inches shorter than I. [J.W. was five feet, eleven inches.] He was delighted with the idea of the trip and my invitation to accompany me on to the National Forest of Akan afterwards but could not seem to speak any English at all in the presence of Nakamura and all the other Japanese. But it was agreed we were to start by train and bus at 4 (it was about 11:30) for a place farther down the peninsula which was our take-off point and where we could stay with a well-to-do fisherman friend of his father's. In the meantime, he invited us to his house for lunch. Nakamura could spend the night there and go back next day to Sapporo.

The house turned out to be a very large one with a big garden court in the centre and occupied by some others besides Tosiro Hamada's family. It was explained that before the war it had been a brothel which accounted for its size. The father, mother and brother all greeted us and preparations were begun for lunch. In the meantime we sat cross legged and talked. The father was a well-to-do farmer who raised race horses. Behind the house was a nice stable and cow barn and a nice trotting course. On the hillside were the pastures.

But all this I did not see until after lunch. They were terribly pleased at the prospect of Tosiro accompanying me and the father put up a fine kakemono which he asked whether I liked. When I assented he said he wanted to give it to me. I was much embarrassed but [Prof.] Nakamura said I should accept and that it was right and proper to do so. He offered to take it back to Sapporo for me.

Then we had a good lunch of rice, raw octopus & other good things and afterwards went out to look at the horses. Some of their colts had been winners. They had two handsome brood mares but their stallion had died recently. There was a colt in one of the box stalls. I was asked whether I would like to ride a horse in the paddock & he was led out. The stirrups were too short so I tried him bareback and found him a little bumptious when I used the stick which they gave me. He was inclined to buck so I was careful for I did not want to fall off in the presence of my hosts. The boys also took a turn but one of them, less cautious than I, soon came flying off. The old father, meantime, in his yukata, was picking wild raspberries of which he gave me a handful. Then we went back to the house for Tosiro to collect his belongings — a few clothes and a huge sack of uncooked rice. The father, meantime, wrote us a long note to his friend, the fisherman.

In one corner of their room, next to the tokonoma, there was a large handsome black lacquer & gold Buddhist altar with religious furnishings and an offering of fruit. Also a picture of the oldest son who had been killed in the war. It turned out to be the anniversary of his death and while we were there a Buddhist priest came in his robes to say some memorial prayers. We all sat respectfully while he lighted a candle, rang the little bell and chanted the holy words in a curious rhythm with a rapid emphasis at the end of each sentence. It was quite impressive.

Then we took our departure & Prof Nakamura walked with us to the station. He is a slight man, a few years older than I and I was really sorry to say goodbye. I felt him to be a real friend and I believe he felt the same warmth towards me.

As we travelled S.W. towards Semani (about 1 hr.) Tosiro began to understand better. He was no longer embarrassed and his ear was getting used to me. From Semani we had to take a bus along the tiny seaside road which was only wide enough, and barely so, for one car.

It was foggy and the waves looked very large as they rose to break on the beach and rock. At intervals there were great limestone bluffs rising straight up from the shore. It was too rough for the boats to be out and they were all hauled up on the beach. The boats there have no engines but I noticed there were windlasses to help worry them up the beach. Men, women and children were out in the edge of the surf gathering the laminaria (brown seaweed) which is used in making soup. They darted out with the receding waves and ran back again laughing as the big waves broke & rolled in.

The house where we stayed was in a little hamlet but was very nice and quite large with yew trees growing in the front yard. There was a charcoal fire in a kind of stove in the kitchen and the inevitable tea kettle was boiling. In the main room there was the usual pit with ashes and an adjustable hook of brass hanging from the ceiling for the kettle. A great-great grandmother was sitting by it, 95 years old, impassive as a Bodisatva. She was deaf and somewhat blind. The house was on the edge of the beach & we could hear the thunder of the waves breaking & see them through the partly open shoji. While we were waiting for the master to come home we walked along the beach watching the seaweed fishers and looking at the wooden boats.

When the master came there was great talk about the crossing of the mountains. There was a great deal said about the bears which I could not take seriously but which the others seemed to do. It was agreed however that we could not possibly go without a guide and that there was but one who knew the way, namely "the guard of the mountain," as Tosiro called him, or, as we should say, forest ranger. Our host went out to arrange with him & came back to report that he would be on hand at 7 o'clock in the morning with his gun as a defense against bears; people had been killed by bears on the path we were to take. So we had supper and a primitive form of sake which is the white fermented paste of rice, not the usual liquid. And so to bed, side by side on the futons (their mattresses) spread on the floor in the inner room. And up at six for a stroll along the beach to watch the seaweed fishers, who were already at work, until breakfast was ready. It was an ample breakfast with raw sea urchins' eggs among other good things. Soon our guide appeared and we took leave of our host.

It was a hard day — one of the hardest walks I have had. It was only 18 miles and by good fortune the last 2 or 3 miles were cut off by a ride. But the 15 miles took nearly 12 hours. It was very beautiful as we followed up a rushing river where we swam twice and beside which we lunched on cold rice — the usual lunch. The mountains were partly hidden in clouds but at times we had a bright hot sun. Near the pass the path vanished completely and our guide wandered in vain. It was gone and we had to make our way through a tangle of bamboo grass (Sassa grass) often 8 or 10 feet high. It was like climbing through Grandma Cabot's big yew tree. We slipped and fell & stuck but at last we were on the pass and could see the blue Pacific on the other side. Coming down was worse than going up and we were all very tired. I was so tired that I slipped & fell often. Also I got terribly stung by some kind of nettle and my ankles are now twice their usual size.

It was really a race as to whether we should get out of the rough country before dark but we won it and, after a last section of thicket, found ourselves on a real road. To our delight, a lumber truck laden with logs showed up just at that moment and we hailed it and jumped aboard & so saved 2 - 3 miles.

Please give my love to Aunt Susan, Uncle Charlie, Charlie jr. & Ben & any others you may see & tell them of my doings & of course give them my letters to read if they are interested. Farmy

---

August 7, 1950   *Gift Refused*
                                    JW in Sendai to Marblehead

Dear Anne & Jeff, This is a roll of Jap note paper which I bought in Aomori & which is very good for air mail. I hope I am not boring you with these long accounts of my doings. They are so different from anything that happens at home that I think you may want to hear of them.

My last letter, which was finished on the ferry from Hokkaido to Aomori got me to the coast with Tosiro and the guide, terribly tired after crossing the mountains. We were thankful indeed for the clean hospitality of the little inn in the fishing village on the coast. It was nearly dark when we got there and we were shown into a spotless room opening across the usual gallery onto an orchard garden. A cosy hanging oil lamp was lighted over the fireplace (a pit full of snowy white sifted ashes) where a charcoal fire was started to get the tea boiling. While supper was making we had a good wash (for once there was no bath), put on spotless fresh yukatas and sat down cross legged to drink our tea, which certainly went to the right spot. The shoji were partly drawn and we had a great sense of well being. Then came a good supper, with some especially nice roasted river fish, and we treated ourselves to some hot sake, 5 of their little bottles which we drank from the tiny china cups. By the time supper was over we were ready for beds, which we ordered to be brought. The guide slept in one room and Tosiro and I in the room where we had eaten.

We were to be up at 5 in order to have breakfast and be underway by the daily bus along the coast road soon after 6. It was good to see the blue sky and white clouds over the big mountains when we opened our eyes before going to wash and get dressed. After breakfast we bade farewell to the inn and walked through the little town & down on to the beach while we waited for the bus to be ready. There was some fog as we drove along the narrow shore road cut out of the base of the towering cliffs and we looked through it at the sun lighting up the incoming waves. Here and there the shore widened enough to give room for a fishing village and everywhere the seaweed fishers were at work. In some places too the boats were working their nets just outside the breakers and among the ledges.

We travelled so for nearly 3 hours until we got to the beginning of the railway where we boarded the 3rd class carriage for Obihiro, which you will see on the map. The train was crowded as usual. One man had some delicious fresh king crabs on which we all had a feast until I felt my stomach bulging. I was of course a great curiosity and I must have signed my name almost a dozen times for various passengers. At Obihiro we had a 3 hr. wait and passed the time on the bank of the river, eating our cold rice. We also napped in the grove of a shrine where there was shade, for it was very hot. There too we had quite an adventure owing to my efforts to get through a telephone call to Tokyo. We ended up in the office of the chief official, where something terrible seemed to happen to Tosiro's English so that everything became a complete enigma. Finally, after tea was served all round to the 4 or 5 people present, it was agreed that a telephone call was impossible and I sent a telegram instead.

We were glad enough to get seats in the 3rd class carriage to Kushiro and I was fascinated all the way as I watched the passing hills, the glimpses of sea in passing the coast and the expanse of fields and pastures where there were fine horses.

At Kushiro we had just two minutes to make our connection but we made it and had four final hours to get up to a small mountain town called Toshikuga where there is a hot sulphur spring and which is quite a resort of the Japanese. We put up there at quite a big hotel on the edge of the lake where there is a huge bath, big enough to swim in. We had two nice adjoining rooms, one for sleeping, one for eating, and a balcony. We were glad of a late supper & to get to bed after a hot bath. Next morning we bathed again, all the people going in together, although men & women have separate dressing rooms. It was quite amusing to see a young baby going in with its mother who washed it and comforted it and quieted its howling very nicely. Another woman was washing her hair with the aid of her young daughter. There are wooden buckets with which you bail water out of the pool, while you sit on a low wooden stool and soap and wash yourself thoroughly. Then you must wash off every scrap of soap and dirt before you get into the hot water.

That morning we walked up to a very beautiful crater lake about 4 mi long with an island in the middle. It was only 6 miles to walk but we were so tormented by the flies on the way that we were nearly crazy, and when at last we saw a little shelter house overlooking the lake, we made a run for it. We were glad enough to get a ride back with some Japanese engineers in their car.

That afternoon we bade farewell to our hotel and boarded a bus (there is 1 a day) for Lake Akan which lies at the foot of some volcanic peaks and has a fairy book kind of shore line. We made a little trip by boat on the lake and the next day I did some sketching until noon when we lunched and prepared for the bus which carried us down to the R.R. I may say that the drive up to Lake Akan is one of the really exciting mountain drives, through virgin forest and very wild gorges, that I have seen, & I enjoyed it much as I hate the internal combustion engine.

On the way beyond to the R.R. we had a girl who was suffering from a heart attack which had apparently been brought on by climbing one of the mountains. The poor thing was lying on a stretcher in the frightfully hot overcrowded bus, being jolted over the rough road. Tosiro referred to her as an "illness man." His English was often very ludicrous and he was forever confusing the sexes. At one hotel when a pretty girl who caught his eye brought in our supper he turned to me and said "How - do - you - like - Him?" which struck me as absurd. But I grew more and more fond of his outgoing friendly personality, his sense of humor, his vitality and his good sportsmanship. He wanted to do everything for me — pack and carry my bag, wash my shirt in the evening etc etc — and had to be restrained. When I went to the bath he would bail buckets of hot water under my seat lest I feel cold.

Our last meal together was at a little hotel at Bihoro where we had 3 hours to wait and while away the time by a bath and a leisurely supper in yukatas. We both felt sad at the thought of parting next morning (and a little sad, too, at the anticipation of sitting up all night in a Japanese R.R. car.) We had some sake together in the train which helped us to sleep, and awoke next A.M. to find the train would be very late owing to a washout. We all had to get out and walk 300 yds over an improvised bridge & get onto another train smaller than the first. When I thought we were packed as tight as it was possible to be, they put up ladders to the windows and stuffed in the last remaining stragglers, mainly women.

I had two days left in Sapporo. The morning of the first I spent at the chem. laboratory & in the P.M. Tosiro came to see me, bringing his best friend, also a football player, with whom he was staying for several days in Sapporo. There was then a very funny incident. I knew how much Am. cigarettes meant to Japanese people so I had just bought my quota of a carton and had half of it ready for Tosiro & his friend. This was offered after they had been with me about 1/2 hr. They soon, to my surprise, said they had guests coming and must leave at once. They took neither the cigarettes nor some olives and chocolates which I had got for them. I knew something was wrong and finally got the girl in the hotel to reach them by telephone & tell them I was sorry they had forgotten their cigarettes and hoped they would come & get them. Sure enough they came over at 6 with a note which I enclose explaining they had thought it impolite to take such a large gift from "a superior person" but realized American standards were different & took the cigarettes.

We spent the evening together very pleasantly. They were very resentful of the relations of G.I.s & Japanese street girls in Sapporo & took me down one of the more disorderly streets to show me what went on. I can't blame them for feeling so but of course, as I told them, all soldiers are like that.

Next morning I spent with Dr. Higashi who has done some work very much like my own & made use of some of my results. In the afternoon, after another sci-visit, I went to tea with Udzumasa & his family. He was a baron under the old regime and had been in U.S.A. & Europe. His wife & 20-year old daughter were charming &, from her photgraphs as a bride of 19, the mother was like the daughter of today. They had baked a European cake for me & had some fruit and they showed me an album of photographs of their trip to U.S.A. But the chief exhibit was the wife's kimonos, dating from her wedding day. She put them on her daughter who showed them off to great advantage. With 20 or so kimonos and half a dozen or a dozen obis, the number of combinations and permutations is enormous, although of course all do not go together.

When I got back to the hotel I was quite touched to find a bottle of salve for my itching ankles which Tosiro had taken the trouble to get from the university hospital. I had dinner with Col Switzer & drove to the station where Tosiro & his friend were waiting to see me off.

The trip to Sendai should have been 24 hrs but turned out to be 48 due to the terrible floods in Honshu resulting from a typhoon in that region. The five-hour crossing on a sparkling sea with a brisk wind was delightful. I wrote a large part of my last letter to you on the boat. But at Aomori we found the occupying forces train to Tokyo had had to be rerouted down the coast about to Niigata. Many troops with guns and tin hats were on the move from the north down to the Kyushu area on the way to Korea, all I think a little keyed up.

My traveling companion was an army captain of rather limited parts but very nice. He had an enlisted man with him from Lowell,

Mass., who had had his forefinger bitten off in a fight with another G.I. and promptly got lost in Aomori and was never seen by us again. We had the option of going all the way to Tokyo with the dubious possibility of a train back to Sendai or a round-about cross-country trip from Niitzu (near Niigata) to Karyama almost on the opposite side of Japan via a cross-country line & so by an uncertain route to Sendai. I chose the latter and so did the captain & a sergeant with two enlisted men with tin hats and tommy guns. We all travelled together. I took them to a country inn at Niitzu where we cut a rather ludicrous figure & I wonder what the Japanese thought as I came in followed by this armed guard. They were as courteous & obsequious as ever. The captain & I had our beds laid out side by side — the others elsewhere. He could not eat any of the Jap. food at breakfast except 2 eggs, which made me feel very scornful. They were all armed with sandwiches.

The trip next day across country to Karyama was most beautiful, up some deep river gorge, heavily wooded, with ancient groups of houses and small villages scattered about and the peasants moving here and there in medieval clothes. The big hats and grass rain capes are most arresting. At Karyama we changed to a train for Fukushima where we took a bus to circumvent a washout and then got another train to Sendai.

I will stop here. I have written enough for 1 envelope. I am back in Tokyo & was delighted to get your letter, Anne, and to hear your affairs at Radcliffe are on such a good footing. They have certainly met you more than half way and I hope you can pass the exams & be a junior. As for you, Jeff, I gather the Math is pretty tough. I know many seniors & even graduate students find it so. I hope you can take it. Don't be afraid to ask for help and remember that formulating your difficulties almost answers them in many cases. And take some time off for relaxation. I fear the heat is horrid but I suspect it is nothing to what I meet here. Hereafter address me:

JW

E.S.S. Sci & Tech

G.H.Q. SCAP

APO 500 c/o Postmaster, San Francisco

Lots & lots of love Farmy

August 11, 1950   *Pacific Coast at Sendai*
                              JW in Sendai to Marblehead

Dear Anne & Jeff, This is to bring you up to date on my doings. I think my last letter took me to Sendai. The situation there is much more military than in Sapporo. It was a little confusing at the station & one of my bags, the one with my paints in it, was missing. (It has since caught up with me.) But I ran across the colonel who arranged for a billet for me in the guest house at the camp on a hill overlooking the city.

Sendai is one of the old medieval cities of Japan but was largely burned in the war. I had the regular type of B.O.Q. supper, stopped in at a movie for a time afterwards and then went to bed. It all reminded me of the last war. Next morning I went down to the Civil Affairs Office with the colonel & then drove on to the university where I was taken to the laboratory of old Prof Tominaga, the physical chemist. He took me round to see various people until lunch time when I drove back to the camp. In the P.M. they all assembled in a lecture room and asked me to make a speech, which I did, first about my feelings about Japan and then about my work on hemoglobin. Afterwards there was a rather inadequate discussion and a little awkwardness until it was suggested that I would like to see some of the valuable makimonos and block prints belonging to the university. So after a hasty visit to the laboratories of organic chemistry we all, or rather quite a group of us, trooped over to the library where they put on a very fine show.

There were some really beautiful loosely done horizontal scroll paintings (makimonos) of the Tokugawa period showing a series of figures. Then there was an ancient book illustrating the process of silver mining in [the southern island of] Kyushu and finally a complete and superb set of Hiroshigi's prints of the old road from Tokyo to Kyoto — about 45. They are overwhelmingly beautiful. There was an equally fine set of Hokusai's small but possibly more subtle views (36) of the same subject. Next day I got 2 jeeps & took 4 of the university folk out to Matsushima Bay, about 1 hr's drive from Sendai, where there is a large oyster fishery and which is supposed to be one of the

3 most beautiful spots in Japan with its "804" islands. It was certainly very beautiful and had much of that fairy-tale, doll-like character which is so characteristic of Honshu.

We stopped at a medieval fishing town on the way and visited the shrine or temple (I forget which) where many sailors go to insure success and protection. The very narrow streets lined with dark little shops and the glimpses of family life inside were hardly adequate for our jeeps. On the limestone shores of the bay there were various caves and grottos where Buddhist monks used to sit for long periods without food or sleep. We had lunch and tea at a kind of tea house on the top of a hill overlooking the bay and then one jeep with two of the professors went home. The rest of us got a fishing boat with one scull oar & one sail to take us out for a spin on the bay. The water was very yellow with mud due to the recent typhoon and it was extremely hot (over 90 in the shade) but we had a little awning which helped. I tried driving the boat with the curious scull and found it quite easy.

On the way home we stopped at a small farming hamlet where there was a very old farmhouse. The whole family were there, much mystified by the appearance of a jeep, but they were most cordial and asked us in. The house had been partly flooded in the recent typhoon and everything was out in the farm yard drying. Some of the polished floor boards had been taken up. (You see, since no one ever uses shoes on the floors and they are polished everyday without any application of oil or varnish, they have the smoothness and sheen of a dull mirror.) Such houses have no chimney and the huge sprawling beams are deep black.

In Sendai we stopped to see a silk thread factory and the ruins of the old Daimyo's palace on the hill (The Daimyos of Sendai, named Date, were the 3rd most powerful family in Japan up to the Meiji revolution, so I am told. The first was of course the Tokugawas & the second that of the Daimyos of Kanazawa. Mrs. Miura's maternal grandfather was, I believe, the last Daimyo of Kanazawa and became Marquis Macoda after the revolution in 1868.)

In the evening I went to supper with the Fujisus. Their pre-war house is occupied by an army officer and they live in a rather second-rate affair but nice enough. Their 14-year old boy already spoke a little English and was quite up-and-coming. He had constructed a model R.R. with great skill. They were all delightful and gave me a perfect feast with a bottle of French wine. I was sent home in the university car at 11. Next day I spent talking to a brilliant young professor of organic chemistry and to a still younger physical and biological chemist and in the evening boarded the train for Tokyo where I arrived yesterday. The Fujisus came to see me off.

In the P.M. I had a talk with Mizushima and Miura about plans. I have been invited to visit and lecture at most of the main universities next autumn & cannot of course fit everything in. I have arranged to lecture at Tokyo in October & shall probably be at Kyoto-Osaka in Nov. and in Kyushu part of December. In the meantime I am off on Sunday for 5 or 6 days with the Miuras at Mrs M's father's farm on the way to Sendai & then I go on to Niigata to lecture & see some fireworks & then on a long trek to Kyoto, Osaka, Nagoya & Hiroshima. J.W.

Aug 18, 1950   *Old Farm at Nasu*
                            JW in Tokyo to Marblehead

Dear Anne & Jeff, I believe the last you heard of me was my getting back to Tokyo from Sendai. I had a few letters and reports to write and plans to make of things to come and then I left on my visit to the country with Miura's parents-in-laws. But while in Tokyo I had a nice dinner with the Miuras & Dr. Mizushima & also an afternoon at the Kabuki play with the the two Miuras & their sister-in-law. I saw the white heron dance, symbolizing the life of woman. On one of the evenings there was a farewell party at Maj Taylor's for 2 of the E.S.S. people who were leaving. We all drove out to the Taylors' little army house where there was a bar set up with the greatest array of bottles you ever saw. We had a stand-up supper, some games, movies & color photographs, a little dancing & I got back to the hotel at 12:30. The last evening I spent with [Prof.] Nakamura.

On Sunday Aug 13 at 8:30 I called for the Miuras: Yoshiaki, Reiko & the two girls (aged 2 & 5) & we drove to Ueno Station where there were rivers of people flowing in every direction and where although we got into line long before the gates were open, we had barely time to get seats in the 2nd class carriage (there is no first class). It was a 3 hours' trip to the little station about 1/2 or 1/3 of the way to Sendai where we alighted — all through the expanse of rice fields and gardens. At the station we were met by a man servant with mustaches and a species of short riding boot who hurried off to fetch the charcoal burning motor car which drove us 10-12 miles along a narrow country road into the very heart of rural Japan. We passed one town of some size and then a few hamlets and turned in between 2 slender limestone gateposts under a great arch of trees — cool and welcome after the heat and dust of the road. We found ourselves in a kind of farmyard or courtyard with a long rambling wooden house on one side, trees & various farm buildings on the other. Of these the most notable was the great storage barn of cut limestone, used to keep the rice crop.

Our bags were carried in and we entered the two open rooms facing us. By day, when the shoji are pushed back, a Japanese house is like a doll's house with the front taken off. The floor is raised up about 2 steps above the level of the ground and of course you shed yr. shoes before you step on the polished wooden floor of the gallery or passage-way in front of the main rooms. There are two sets of shoji, one to separate the rooms from the gallery and one the gallery from the outside. The two rooms were really one, for the screens separating them had been taken away for summer. It was some time before the parents made their appearance. In the meantime we arranged the presents we had brought — candy, cocoa etc — very much as at Xmas with us. The parents said what they wanted, just as we do for a birthday or at Christmas. We also had a chance to look about. In the tokonoma there was a beautifully arranged bowl of wild flowers, a handsome kakemono which I was told was the work of the old count, and a magnificent low table and box of writing materials in gold lacquer, bearing the imperial crest of the chrysanthemums & evidently the gift of an emperor. In the middle of the room there was a large square red lacquered table which was to be our dining table. Presently the parents & sister-in-law came in. The old Count Hirata was a rather wizened yellow man with birdlike eyes and black short-cropped hair, very thin, very active, very positive and quite imperious, of 70 years. He made me think, both in appearance and manner of speech, of the Samurai of the Kabuki plays. He was a most interesting character as it proved.

Before the war he had been very rich and the number of his dependants on this one estate was about 1000, divided into about 150 households. He had been quite deaf from early childhood and in consequence had taken up painting and been director of the Academy of Art in Tokyo, painting in the classical manner. He had also written poetry (like all cultivated Japanese) but (unlike most) had published 2 books of verse. He was full of eccentricities and vanity. He had a large house in Tokyo, one by the sea near Kamakura and a villa in the mountains. He had maintained one of the largest and most conspicuous cars in Tokyo but always insisted on traveling 3rd class on the train. He regarded himself as the leading contemporary Japanese painter. If he did not like a guest, he would confine himself to his room during the visit. Now of course his money was largely gone, as with all upper class Japanese, as a result of the enforced reforms, and he had retired to what was left of his farm — a modicum of what it had been — with his wife & widowed daughter of 32 and little grandson — and was up with the birds, feeding his hens, tending his vines, supervising his rice fields and never resting for a moment.

His grandfather had been a simple Samurai from the N.W. of Japan and had been adopted and somehow or other (I am not sure just how) had been sent to Germany for an education just after the Meiji era and taken a leading part in the codification of the laws. He had in consequence become very rich and acquired a title and the estate where I was visiting, and no doubt many other sources of wealth. The son, father of my host, had been chancellor under the last emperor. The [present] Count paid relatively little attention to his children but seemed more interested in me, as a stranger. I was the first Westerner he had ever had as a guest anywhere and the first to visit that remote district of Japan, and he was quite excited and had made many plans to show me Japanese life.

His wife I recognized at once to be a delightful and remarkable woman — about 60 — 10 years younger than her husband, stout with her straight black hair combed back from her forehead in the old Japanese manner, smiling, executive in her grandmotherly way, dressed in a blue & white kimono of simple pattern with the usual obi and in bare feet like all of us. She was a gifted woman — a skillful painter, an able woodcarver, quite intellectual and the manager of the family. She came from one of the proudest, richest and oldest families of Japan, the Maedas, lords of Kanazawa since the days of Hideyoshi. Her father had been a viscount, one of the younger branches of the family but, when her father died in her early girlhood, she and her brother and sister had been taken on by the old Marquis, head of the family, and the brother had been adopted as heir of the main line in default of a son. So she had grown up in the old palace, behind the red lacquered gate, now a national treasure and leading into the main grounds of the Imperial University, which formerly constituted the Daimyo's garden. Later the Marquis gave his place for the founding of the university and received in exchange the tract of land at Komba, now the grounds of the Institute of Science and Technology.

The Maedas were second only to the Shogun and had financed the Meiji revolution in large part. But you would not have associated her with such grandeur if you had seen her in her oldest clothes going out to tend the hens, or bringing a tub of water to me in the bath, or taking part in cooking over the tiny wooden brazier. I think the old Count, for all his dominating manner, was secretly galled at the dominating character of his wife. He once said to his son-in-law Yoshiaki "if you ever marry again, do not chose too strong a woman." But they were a happy and remarkable couple. They expressed great satisfaction in the pile of presents that were carried off to their quarters.

Reiko had brought a lunch of sandwiches for us and this we now brought out. Tea was brought in and some delicious home-grown tomatoes and other things which I forget after many feasts and we all sat on the floor round the red table. I duly admired the contents of the tokonoma, which involved no hypocricy you may be sure, and was shown in detail the exquisite writing case (you will see such in the collection of gold lacquer at the Boston Museum, a low table about 24" by 14" by 4" high and a box containing ink stone, writing brushes etc.).

Then Yoshiaki and I were taken out by the old Count to see his hens, the dogs, the beloved vegetables, the garden much in need of care with its little pond, its shrubs, its maples and other trees, its tiny bridge and, in a far part, the bamboo house built to house the

Emperor when he had visited the estate to see the growing of rice some years previously. There were some large slate monuments with commemorative inscriptions, one in honor of the first bailiff, one (as I remember) containing something about the Emperor's visit. (That of course was an overwhelming honor). Afterwards, as I had expressed a great interest in the farming, we set out on a walk over the rice fields and round about through the farms, each with its trees, its outbuildings, and something of a garden and clipped hedges, some of them of tea plants, some very tall & of cedar. It was all like a chess board with streams running between the squares, the squares often distorted, and with the farm buildings at the corners and footpaths and byways crossing the whole. We stopped at several places and were greeted deferentially by the farmers and their wives who would bow low to us, sometimes kneeling on the floors of their houses and touching their heads to the ground.

At one place we were given tea; at another tea supplemented by fresh roasted corn. As I say, no foreigner had been in this district within memory of man and this was a great occasion. It was a great occasion also for me. This was about the nearest thing to pre-Meiji Japan I had seen. The old man seemed not the least bit tired, his bright little eyes sparkling like the eyes of a sparrow hawk, which he much resembled. He wore a huge straw hat, a white cotton shirt, thin brown trousers and light shoes with the big toe separate from the others like a mitten. [2 drawings] (Such are very common everywhere in Japan.) He took us up a long flight of steps to a shrine on a hilltop where the hair of his famous grandfather was buried. Other parts of the great man were buried elsewhere.

Then we returned home in time for Yoshiaki and me to be par-boiled in the wooden bath tub next the kitchen where supper was making, before we put on our yukatas and obis. Supper was cooked by the widowed daughter who was very much in the background. Yoshiaki said neither of the women would eat with us, which indeed they did not unless perhaps the old Countess on our first night (I am not quite sure but I believe she only knelt beside us to fill the glasses with sake). But Reiko sat with us & of course the old Count in his striped blue & white yukata. We had the most varied and wonderful meals, for the sister was a most versatile cook. The little Japanese eggplants are about the most delicious vegetables I have ever eaten.

After supper and drinking to each other, the shamisen or 3-stringed lute was brought out & the two sisters knelt side by side and, after a low bow to us, played and sang duets to us, many containing parts of the songs of Noh dances. The 3 children, meantime, were still up (one being the sister's boy of 4. He seemed to be hardly weaned and was constantly trying to suck from his mother. The grandfather, looking on, said "you should use a bitter extract to stop such habits"). And then a servant came to close the shoji and our beds, two for the Miura family, one for me, were laid out on the floor and two great mosquito bars, just like those shown in some of the Hokusai prints, were suspended over them and we lay down to sleep in our yukatas. It is the way of the country.

The W.C. was at one end of a long passage, past a servant's room where there was a sewing machine. It had a light door with a sliding latch opening into an ante room from which two doors opened, one for the lesser, one for the greater function. A pair of straw slippers were at the threshold as is usual, so that one's bare feet may not touch the floor of the latrine, spotless as it is. One of the inner rooms has a slitlike opening in the floor over which you squat, according to the universal custom of the East. (I am always in great terror of losing one of my loose-fitting sandals in getting into position over this slit. So far that has not happened to me.) The other inner room has a urinal.

In the night I awoke in the pitch blackness of the sealed house, wanting to relieve myself. I wondered whether I dared trust myself to the maze of passages, whether I should go crashing into something if I did, or whether I should be so lost as never to regain my bed again. But I braved it, crawled out from under the mosquito bar and groped my way past the room where I could hear the heavy breathing of the servant woman and to my delight and relief finally felt my hand to be on the sliding latch of the object of all my ambitions. Soon I was in bed again.

When I awoke, I heard the cocks crowing and the household stirring but not the Miuras. I took my wash things to the sink next to the bathroom where the sister brought me a tea kettle of hot water and the old Countess was supervising various activities as I shaved and brushed my teeth with only my underdrawers. (Later Reiko made me

two sets of loin cloths which I use now in preference.) After my morning ablutions I went back to our rooms to find the shojis open and to see the old Count entering the hen house which faced us. So I put on a pair of getas (wooden sandals with a cord between the great toe and the rest and raised with a kind of clog [drawing showing the heel overhanging the clog] and went to join him.

We Miuras had breakfast by ourselves, brought in by the sister. I may say that before breakfast my host had also taken me on a little tour of the farm buildings: into the storage barn for the rice and other crops; into various tool sheds where the different hoes, forks and mattox & sickles were kept; into the old grist mill driven by a water-wheel now rotted away; into the servants' hall where 4 household servants were busy eating rice; into the manure barn where, among other things, there was a well for rotting human night-soil, not at all as objectionable as you might imagine.

After an ample breakfast with its rice, seaweed, smoked fish, pickled cucumbers, soup made of tofu and fermented soy beans etc, etc, which we ate in yukatas, the old Count brought out his painting equipment — ink slab & ink, many brushes, different kinds of paper and some of his own works as examples. They were all of flowers. He also showed us his colors — pigments in vials — but he only intended to use black and white. There was a big porcelain jar divided into two sections for water and a kind of felt saddle cloth as a protection to prevent the paint getting on to the tatami. He was very deft and I felt most incompetent in trying to achieve the fleshy part of an eggplant with one single sweeping motion of a big brush loaded more heavily on one side than the other. An exact judgment as to the necessary wetness of the brush in relation to the texture of the paper was most difficult and baffling to achieve. I spent the morning at it and then, dripping from the heat, had a cold bath before lunch.

After lunch I was to give a "lecture," of the Count's arranging, to a group of his erstwhile principal tenant farmers. It was to be held in a kind of club house or grange at one part of the premises. We were to assemble at 1:00 but it turned out to be 2:40 before the principal farmer came to report that all was ready. In the meantime I had a deep nap in the overwhelming moist heat of midday. When I entered the hall the assembled farmers were all in the formal kneeling position. I was given a chair to sit in and had been instructed by the Count to wear my American clothes. He and Yoshiaki, who was to be the interpreter, were in their yukatas. The farmers were fanning themselves and I was dripping wet. My wretched nylon shirts absorb no water. I was told to speak for an hour. In the meantime the old Count made an introduction. I did not know quite what to say but began by telling of my first impressions of Japan, then gave a little sketch of my past doings in the country and some reflections on Japanese life in the city and country. I spoke slowly and had to wait for Yoshiaki to interpret, but the audience sat in rapt attention, listening to every word of my commonplaces as though I had been Demosthenes and showing, it seemed to me, a wonderful sense of humor by their smiles at my poor attempts at humor. They were a fine looking lot and won my heart as a group just as the few we had seen the afternoon before had done individually.

When I ceased they all clapped and when I suggested questions there was no diffidence about their speaking up. They wanted to know every conceivable thing: how I liked Japanese food; how well I slept in Japanese beds; how hard American farmers worked; how much they made; how big their families were; how much dowry they gave with their daughters; whether children working with their parents were paid; how a girl could save up against the days of her marriage; how many people had automobiles in U.S.A.; how many children they had etc. When I explained that marriages were not arranged by parents, one asked in great compassion what happened to the young who could not find mates for themselves. They all regarded U.S.A. as a dream world, where rivers were streams of gold, and were greatly relieved and gratified when I pointed out some of the respects in which I thought Japan was far better off, as in the strength of a family feeling and in the joy and cooperation of family and group work and the beauty of their surroundings.

They wanted to know how the old were provided for in U.S.A. if they did not live with their children. And I, too, asked many questions as to the size of the families, the hours of work, the amount of food enjoyed, the length of time that children were nursed by their mothers (sometimes several years, so they said). It is universal for mothers to nurse their babies in Japan and they were astounded when I told them that the absence of nursing was almost as universal with us. It was one of the best discussions I have ever had in my life and lasted 3 hours without a dull moment or an embarrassing silence. At last it had to be broken off. The old Count, poor man, who could hear nothing, was somewhat disturbed at the length of it and several times came up from the sidelines to ask what was going on & whether I was not becoming tired or being embarrassed by the questions. In the middle of it all, I sent a boy to the house to get some U.S. cigarettes to distribute & that pleased everyone. At the end of the questions they all clapped again and the old Count gave a little speech & we adjourned, Yoshiaki & I to a hot bath before supper.

Apparently the news of the occasion spread far & wide and people came to talk to the Count about it with great enthusiasm so that he was much elated and felt his enterprise to be a great success. At dinner he drank to the speech in sake. The women had heard of it from the servant who had come to fetch tea for me while the discussion was going on. You will be amused to hear of one sequel. I had mentioned the population problem in my own comments and had indirectly raised a question suggesting birth control. One of the household men servants came to ask the women next morning, while I was out, what I regarded as the best method of birth control. He had the impression that eating much protein and fat was the secret, because he had observed the diet of the rich, who often had few children, to abound in these items. Apparently if a farmer is known to go to the city to buy the means of birth control, opinion is so strong against him that he almost has to leave the community. Reiko told me of one woman who got hold of some kind of contraceptive jelly and swallowed it as the proper way of making use of it.

We had another fine supper with sake served in the tiny cups as usual. The meals seemed to repeat and were served in lovely china, some I am sure quite valuable. Most of it was Imari ware from Kyushu but there was one large old Korean bowl, used for cucumbers & tomatoes, which I believe was worth several thousand dollars. It was a gift of the Countess' brother. Most of Japanese table china consists of little dishes, saucers and lacquered cups with covers. Blue is the predominant color of the decorations.

The old Count was greatly elated by the success of his meeting all through the evening, as we sat about in the semi-cool of the gallery. There was more of the shamisen music, but by Reiko alone this time, and outside in the darkness I could see the shadowy figures of the servants listening. Her sister knelt just outside the door leading to the back of the house with the young boy at her breast. None of the children went to bed much before we did.

I forgot to tell you of the wonderful collection of kimonos and obis belonging to the women, which was given the afternoon of our first day (just after we arrived.) One after another, the most magnificent things imaginable, nearly all part of the trousseaux of the daughters, were brought out. The show included their wedding dresses and a resplendent kimono of a stuff whose pattern had been designed by the old Count and which had been made to order in Kyoto. The design was of maple leaves and autumn flowers on a purple ground. But perhaps the most subtle thing was an obi of the old Countess' which dated from her wedding days, I suppose, and which she took occasion to present to Reiko then & there. Reiko said she had never seen it before. It was of very soft subdued colors but the brocade was so heavy it must have been hard to wear. An obi is a very long thing indeed and takes great skill in putting on.

The following day, which was Tuesday, I had been promised a view of the great screen which the old Count had painted or was in the course of painting (for only six panels of the total of 8 were done). It was brought out from a store room, carefully protected by a cloth case. When wide open, the six panels must have been 12 - 14 feet long. The ground was gold and it was covered with a most gorgeous arrangement of autumn flowers in a burst of color. The old man paints mostly flowers though he has done some birds and insects also. Actually I prefer less ornate things but there was certainly nothing crude or in bad taste about this. It began on the left with the same arrangement of maple leaves as the kimono and then proceeded to bursts of chrysanthemums, iris and other things, all very carefully balanced and arranged. The old man said he regarded it as his swan song, and a gorgeous one it was. But later, when he showed me the black and white cartoons for it, I noticed that he had plans for a second screen worked out in complete detail.

After the view of the screen we 3 men set out on a visit to some of the neighboring farms as I had expressed a desire to talk further with the farmers. Yoshiaki and a servant went by bicycle, the old Count walked and I was put on a decrepit horse of ancient days, who could not be got out of a walk though he carried a headstall ornamented with a coronet made of glass like an old-fashioned paperweight. We followed along the byways and finally entered a farmyard where we were greeted by a man I recognized from my audience of the day previous. Men & women — son & daughter-in-law & some others — were busy bringing in the crops on the big carrying frames which they wear on their backs like knapsacks (the old Countess had one). The shoulder straps are of the straw rope which they make with a simple treadle machine. We tied up the horse and sat on the edge of the floor (it is like sitting on the edge of a piazza) without having to take our shoes off. We were brought a most delicious watermelon of yellow flesh, which was irresistable. While we ate, there was quite a long talk about life & manners & then we went on to another farm. Here we were treated in much the same way except that we were given fresh roasted corn and tea in place of the melon. At this place the farmer had a particularly nice garden and many dwarfed pine trees set out in pots. These I was told were a special hobby of his. His father, who was an old old man and a widower, lived in his tiny hut behind the farm house. He was a recluse & preferred to be wholly alone. We had a few words with him, a toothless old man. And then we turned home and retraced our steps over the foot paths, followed by an army of children. I felt like Gulliver in Liliput sitting on the horse.

It was good to have a cold bath before our ample lunch. After it I yielded to sleep with the Miuras on the floor in the overwhelming moist heat and awoke about 3. I kept on my yukata but put on sneakers and borrowed a girl's bicycle to go off sketching by myself. I was anxious to try out some very special Japanese paper which the old Countess had stretched for me. It was very thin and the paint ran on it beyond all control so that my product was a failure but it was given honest criticism and some praise that evening after supper. As on other evenings we had a feast with sake and sat about talking & listening to the shamisen.

Next morning before breakfast the wife of one of the farmers we had visited the day before appeared with a present of roasted eels on bamboo skewers and wrapped in bamboo leaves, which her husband had caught in his wicker eel pots in the rice fields in the night. They are justly regarded as one of the greatest of Japanese delicacies and this was a royal present, prompted by my having expressed my liking for them casually the day before. They were subsequently served up at supper.

In the meantime, the old Count offered to take me sketching by the big river, about two miles off. I was equipped with a newly stretched piece of paper by the Countess, who declared she would provide the paper as long as I would paint, and we set off on foot. The walk down the winding paths, through the fields of rice, tobacco, beans, eggplant, corn, taro and many other crops, and past the hamlets and farms, and over the ditches, and by the men, women & children, was very beautiful but suffocatingly hot. At last we heard the noise of waters and, after a sharp descent between steep banks, found ourselves in the flood plain of the river — white water with a steep line of hills on the far side and with flowers growing in the stony waste of its bed. Half a mile downstream we saw great activity of men and dugouts and headed for it. As we approached we found a dozen or 14 peasants in their loincloths hard at work building a dam for irrigation purposes. Some were poling boats laden with river stones to ballast the structure. Others were in the water lifting big tripods or pyramids of legs into place, or rather taking the weight off them so that the river would sweep them down. Each tripod had a huge basket attached to it into which the ballast was thrown when the structure was set.

I sat down by the edge of the water and started sketching the men but, to my confusion, soon they all became my audience. They were the most wonderful color, burned a dark brown by the sun, and the most lithe & muscular little people you can imagine, strong as possible and some of them beautifully built. It was a fine sight to see a pair of them poling their boats upstream with their green bamboo poles bending to the strain. Pretty soon, to my surprise, I looked up to see the old Count, only his head showing, come shooting down the river unable to stop until well below the dam. Then a little later, when I had about done all I could to a miserable blurred attempt [at a painting], all the others appeared on the scene: the Countess, Reiko & her two children (Michiko & Etsuko) and the sister & her boy. We all went in swimming at this point (even the Countess) and sat on the bank eating apples until at last it was time to start back.

The old Countess set off over the rough stones undaunted, carrying one of the heavy children & the rest of us each with something of a load. When we got back to the path there was a hand cart into which we loaded children, paint bag etc & which Yoshiaki & I took turns dragging. We got home in time for a meal cooked by a servant & far inferior to the usual one. In the afternoon the Countess gave me a long lesson on wood carving until it was time for supper — the supper of the eels (& many other things).

Afterwards we were to go night fishing in the river with two of the house servants. So at dusk 5 of us (Yoshiaki, the Count, I & the boys) set out by a somewhat different way than in the morning. I alone wore shoes rather than getas. The boys carried each a box & a torch and a little spear - like a tiny eel spear. I shall never forget the beauty of that walk between the fields, past the farms & hamlets, through the most devious footpaths. The semicool of the evening; the sense of relaxation of the people after the toil of the day; the sight of them through the hedges eating, washing, sitting in their houses; the sound of their talk and laughter — all with the fading light and the new moon in the West, and later the darkness — went very deep. Several times a boy riding a horse back from the pasture came thundering by in the dark and after him the colt. Several times I had to push the old Count out of the road lest he be struck, for he was deaf.

At length we came to the river where we met a man and a girl and lighted the lamps & put on grass sandals. I waded out with one of the boys and helped hold the glass-bottomed box. I found I was no good at spearing. I lost a sandal in the force of the current and, after I had seen the catching of perhaps a dozen small fish, rejoined the other two on the bank and we set off homewards. The boys stayed till midnight & as a result we had a feast of fried fish the next day. On the way home it was very dark & we got lost but finally regained our sense of direction with the aid of the red light of a midwife's house which served as a lighthouse for a time. The women were waiting up for us with tea & fruit when we got home & we tumbled into bed about 11.

Next day we were to start back in the P.M. but in the morning the

Count had arranged for us to pay a visit to the country doctor, who lived about 1 1/2 - 2 miles away in a tiny hamlet & had been to call on us the morning previous. Yoshiaki & I rode on bicycles. Y. took the old Count up behind him on the baggage rack but the paths were rough & the old man preferred to walk & got down. At the doctor's house we were given beer & cakes and fruit & fresh fish & we had a most interesting talk with him about his patients. About 80% of the children have worms; the women stay at home 10 days after the birth of a child; tuberculosis is the gravest sickness. These were some of the facts. He was a fine man, from Tokyo University, who lived with his wife & parents in an ample house with a beautiful garden & a 2nd story over part of it. His father had had the practise before him. He made his rounds on a motorcycle.

And after that home to lunch where I packed my bag. I had several presents to take (Chinese ink, a golden piece of earring, some pictures & handmade paper) so my bags were full. At the parting we all assembled, some photographs were taken & away we drove, the old Countess & her grandson accompanying us.

I have written too long & will see if I can stuff this into an envelope now. I see the last part reads poorly.

Farmy

August 29, 1950   *A Modern Boatyard*
                                    JW in Nagoya to Marblehead

Dear Anne & Jeff, I am far behind in my correspondence. It is a week since I sent my last letter & the most eventful in many ways that I have had. But let me begin with one or two accounts of interesting Japanese customs.

First as to marriage. In feudal Japan all & even now the vast majority (80 - 90% or more) of all marriages, except perhaps in Tokyo, are arranged by an intermediary who knows both families but not necessarily the proposed spouses. Family, money (dowry) and reported character are the main considerations. Among the class of people I see the most of, the man is usually 25-27 & the woman 20-23, but among farmers the man may be 20-22 & the woman 18-20.

Divorce used to be very rare but has become more common recently. A widow used never to remarry but there is beginning to be a departure from this custom now. Previously it was the custom for the widow to live with her husband's parents and to be kept much in the background, often almost in the position of a servant. I told you something of the widowed daughter of the Hiratas', aged about 30, who lived with her own parents with her 4 year old son. That was unusual but, as I said, she was much in the background and did nearly all the cooking. Of course women in old Japanese families are scarcely seen by guests although they may serve meals. It was only because of special representations of Yoshiaki (and no doubt curiosity on the women's part) that I saw as much of the Countess and the widowed daughter at Nasu as I did.

Before we arrived there Yoshiaki told me he was anxious as to my impressions of his sister-in-law as compared with his wife Reiko. She was certainly less happy (not unnaturally) and much more cold and ambitious in temperament than Reiko. I judge her marriage with a successful Japanese banker who also had been very ambitious had not been too happy. The husband had contracted tuberculosis in Peking during the war & had subsequently died in Kamakura a couple of years ago. Now the old Count & Countess had withdrawn entirely to the country, life must have become very bleak and thin for the young widow. With the parents' approval, but contrary to all custom, a marriage had been arranged with a childless widower about 40 years old from Osaka. He was rich and successful as president of an electrical Co. which was a subsidiary of a much larger company run by a relative who had adopted one of the Hiratas' younger sons.

Adoption is a custom strange to us and hard to understand of which I will say more presently. Yoshiaki had the impression that the prospective husband was also rather cold & would perhaps be a difficult spouse for his sister-in-law, the more so as the position of women in the Osaka region is more strictly prescribed by custom than in the Tokyo area & they are much more suppressed. The marriage had been negotiated, or was being negotiated, by the older man in Kyoto. There was considerable interest & discussion of it by Yoshiaki & Reiko with the family, as you can imagine, and they told me all about it.

By the time we arrived at Nasu it had virtually been agreed upon & the bride-to-be had made up her mind to it. Though she had never seen the prospective husband, she had had her photograph taken & sent him a print and received his picture in return. The 4-year old son would be adopted by his father's family (I believe an older brother) & would soon leave his mother. The marriage would occur in October (I suppose I shall be asked to it & I shall look forward to seeing it). To us it all seems incredible but I can see the widow must look upon it as the alternative to an otherwise grim future. As Kyoshi Kurahashi remarked, when I told him of it, the only unusual thing is the fact that, as a widow, she is living with her own family and that she is to remarry at all. (His own mother, who has long been the widow of a Japanese diplomat, has of course never remarried.) This forthcoming marriage of the widow is a hybridization of the old & the new. The old Count & Countess rightly feel remarriage is desirable and are anxious to have it arranged as soon as possible. There is some disagreement between them & their oldest son over the question of dowry & they want to settle the matter before they die. There is a good deal of hostility between them and their son due to the fact that he wants to divorce his present wife and marry his mistress. I begin to see the signs of some of the confusion which has beset our own family life creeping into Japan. The relation between girls & boys is much changed & loosened in more sophisticated circles since the war.

The other custom I will try to explain as far as I can is that of adoption. I told you of the forthcoming adoption of the widow's boy at Nasu; I referred to the adoption of one of the boys of the Hiratas' family (of 7 children) in Osaka; and I believe I mentioned in my last letter that the old Countess's brother had been officially adopted and made heir by an earlier Marquis Maeda, lord of Kanazawa. (His son is the present Marquis.) Whenever there is no male heir in a family (rich or poor) it is custom to adopt the son of a friend or relative. Before the War 9/10 of the family property went to the eldest son, whether a farmer or a nobleman. I was astonished to hear that old Kodama, professor of biology in Tokyo, had recently been officially adopted by the widow of his elder brother, & was a very rich man as a result. But the most curious case of adoption involved two of the house servants at Nasu — the two with whom we went torchlight fishing in the river.

The older one (about 26) had recently married a stalwart fine looking wife of about 23 who was also a house servant. Not long before my visit the couple had adopted the other boy, aged 16, who was strong, willing and friendly. I assume there was some reason why they could not expect children but I was perplexed to hear that it was this very husband who had come to ask the women as to what I conceived to be the most effective method of birth control.

The trip back to Tokyo from Nasu was hot and uneventful. We got into Ueno Station about 6 & the Miuras asked me to have supper & pass the night with them instead of going back to my hotel & I gladly accepted. They live in a small post-war house in the garden of old Dr. Miura's very large house not far from the university. This house has now been taken over by SCAP and is the residence of a Lt. Colonel, but old Dr. Miura and his older son & family live in part of it & have the use of the roof which is a delightfully cool place to pass a summer's evening. The older brother's wife is quite attractive & social & I have twice taken her and Reiko to the Kabuki play. She came in to see us as soon as we arrived back & invited us up to the roof after supper, where I spent the evening with Yoshiaki and his brother & his brother's two attractive boys, aged 16 & 18, who speak English. We talked and had cakes & cold tea as the evening wore on. They brought out a handsome memorial volume picturing the Emperor's official visit to Europe when he was crown prince. Old Dr. Miura had been his medical aide and was shown covered with medals in many group photographs. The brother's wife's father was at that time admiral of the Japanese fleet (Admiral Takeshita) & was also one of the Emperor's suite, and was also shown in full regalia. They were quite proud of the pictures, not unnaturally.

Next day I went down to the office and made some arrangements with Dr. Mizushima about my program for the autumn. He brought with him Dean Sugawara of the science faculty of Nagoya University, where I now am as I write this, & I took them both out to lunch. Next day was Saturday & I was fairly busy preparing for my Sunday start on a trip to last about 1 month: Niigata, Kanazawa, Nagoya, Kyoto, Nara, a week's walking, Osaka, Okayama, Hiroshima, Tokyo.

Kyoshi [Kurahashi] came to lunch with me and afterwards we went to see a Noh play but found it over. So we decided to pay a visit to his Uncle's boat yard, which proved most interesting. The uncle is the one I once spent the day with at Kamakura & who had adopted the young girl & her family. He had formerly been an official of the Matsui Co but, like many other high officials, had been purged. His name is Nagaoka & he is son of the well-known old physicist of that name, teacher of Ukawa. Nagaoka now builds occasional yachts, mostly moderate-sized boats — 30 ft overall — & mostly for American officers. Such boats can be built quite cheaply in Japan where very fine woods are available, among others, teak for planking.

When we arrived he was discussing plans for a small ketch according to designs by Hereshoff with such a man and his Japanese girl. When they left he took us down to the site of construction of a large ketch — 36 feet on the deck — also according to Hereshoff's design. She was just starting and we saw the interesting ceremony of the exorcision of all evil spirits & omens by a Shinto priest in his robes. The priest uttered many solemn words, clapped his hands at important moments, placed some green branches by the ship and beat the air with other branches in order to whip away the spirits as you might whip away mosquitos on a summer evening. This ceremony will prevent accidents and mishaps to the workmen during the course of the construction & will ensure a fortunate career for the ship. It is a very general kind of ceremony for the Japanese & without it, the workmen would not be happy. After it the owner, Col. Glenn, showed up with a Japanese woman & some cigarettes & sake with which to furnish the table that was set out with cakes & savories such as dried squid. He asked me if I would like to go sailing with him at Yokohama when I get back.

Then we took leave & walked back to the hotel where I had a shower & changed my clothes in preparation for dinner with Bunker. B's car picked me up at 8 and we stopped for Nora Walu [?] as I may have written you. She was at the Press Club and has been correspondent in Korea. We 3 had a pleasant dinner at which she talked of her experiences in Korea & earlier in China and I went home to bed.

Next morning I was up at 6 to pack & drive to Ueno Station to meet Miura, who was to make the trip with me as far as Nagoya. The drive was a most distressing preliminary to our trip as the car broke down halfway to the station & I feared the worst. But the Japanese driver (from G.H.Q.) rose to the occasion, opened the hood and had the engine running in a jiffy. Then at the station I found I had still to get an official travel request, so I had to summon another car from the G.H.Q. motor pool & dash off to the centre of Tokyo & back before I could get my tickets. But I made it and, after a long but beautiful journey of 7 hrs right across Japan & over the mountains, reached Niigata in the late afternoon.

I will say no more in this letter but tell you of what followed upon arrival at Niigata in my next. Tomorrow I am off for the Ise Penninsula & then to Kyoto. Tell Hisako when you see her that I am looking forward to seeing her sister in Osaka.

Yr. devoted Farmy

Sept 2, 1950   *Fireworks at Niigata*
                                              JW in Kyoto to Marblehead

Dear Anne & Jeff, I must try to catch up on the account of what I have been doing. My last letter took me to Niigata where I arrived with Yoshiaki Miura 2 weeks ago tomorrow, very hot & dirty about 5:30 p.m. We were met at the station by Prof. Shimazono, the biochemist and Secretary to the University, in the university car. Niigata was a medical school of some age & standing but, as a university, is a post-war creation under the much-opposed program put over (unwisely I suspect) by SCAP.

I was taken at once to the army billet, where all Americans on official travel orders are put up, and Yoshiaki went to spend the night with the Shimazonos (S. married his cousin.) The place where I stayed was the residence of the Japanese pre-war millionnaire — a great big American-style house in bad taste but airy & with a fine view. A dozen or more males are housed & fed there. They are nearly all connected with counter-intelligence (C.I.C.) whose function seems to be primarily to watch for communist activities. It was not very comfortable for I had a bed in a large room with several others & there was only one bathroom for all of us. But it was friendly and informal and I was interested in the point of view of our people in such a small provincial city. On the whole they are a nice crowd & like where they are but most of them live isolated from the life of Japan by a crust of Americanisms & U.S. prejudices which they carry everywhere. After supper I took a stroll and then Shimazono & his wife & Yoshiaki came in to pay me a visit. I gave them some beer and then we all set out to have a look at the town.

It is a small provincial city, with between one & two hundred thousand people, and a port. It is situated in a rich farming area which was famous before the war for its great landlords. The district might be called the Holland of Japan, for it is low & flat, and many of the rice fields lie below the level of the two rivers which join at Niigata, and have been reclaimed by means of dikes & pumps. The city itself is permeated by canals, which gives it quite a charming effect. There are many narrow streets lined with old fashioned houses characteristic of the district. Yoshiaki said it is noted for the beauty of its women and has a corresponding number of restaurants, geisha girls and places of entertainment. Certainly there were also innumerable inns.

We all walked up to a restaurant at the top of one of the two or three tall European buildings in the centre of town & had a look about & then strolled through the streets until we came to the house of an old doctor, who had formerly been rector of the university when it was purely a medical school and was a friend of old Dr. Miura. The son & daughter were there also & they gave us refreshments and much cordiality. The old man presented me with one of his flower paintings.

Next day my program was to be taken to a very beautiful kind of manor house an hour's drive away, which was now opened as a museum and where there was a fine collection of porcelain, though the family still lived in part of the house. Then at 1:00, I was to give a two hour lecture with the aid of an interpreter and after a chance to talk with the laboratory people in the latter part of the P.M., go to a dinner given by the rector in the evening. So in the morning I was picked up by Miura, Shimazono & his wife and an authority on porcelain and taken on a lovely drive into the country, through some medieval-looking villages, along the banks of one of the big rivers until at last we arrived at the gate of our destination. The village architecture in the Niigata district is rather different from that of other parts &, in the larger villages, there are overhanging eaves to allow for a passageway clear of snow along the side of the street, for the snow lies very deep in W. and N.W. Japan in winter. A little inland from Niigata it may lie 6 - 8 ft deep in mid winter; but in summer the climate is extremely hot and sultry and a great proportion of the working men were clad only in loin cloths. People gave a sense of languidness and some of the women appeared bare to the waist.

At our destination we crossed a huge gravel courtyard, partly covered by the much-prized moss of Japan, to the large low manor house, about 130 years old, where we were greeted by the younger brother, the owner himself being away. It was a very big house indeed one of the biggest I have seen in Japan and before the war the estate had boasted about 3000 tenants on its rice fields, say 15,000 - 20,000 dependants. I believe it was one of the very biggest of Japan. The household servants alone numbered about 30. It had some beautiful gardens and a tea house belonging to it and a very fine collection of old Sado ware & other porcelains as well as some nice kakemonos. We were shown the old kitchens, the office, the place where a court was held to deal with minor misdemeanors, and were taken around the gardens. But we had to start back without seeing the farm buildings on account of my lecture.

We did not get back to the rector's office until about 1 but he insisted on my having some lunch which was brought in and, as a result of which, the affair started 1/2 hour late. He and Dr. Shimazono each made an introduction & Yoshiaki acted as interpreter. It is very frustrating to have to talk through an interpreter and when it was over I had a great sense of failure. But I believe they all got something from it. It was a very steep amphitheater, characteristic of the medical tradition. Later there were some questions & discussion & then we adjourned to the rector's office again for tea & continued discussion. The dinner was a very convivial affair in the European style at a city restaurant where we had some interesting general talk. Afterwards Yoshiaki & I walked home to my quarters.

Next day I was to give another 2 hr. lecture as before, but some other doings were arranged for the morning and in the evening there were to be some famous fireworks on the river which, thanks to Yoshiaki, I was able to see from a boat — a very much coveted privilege. Yoshiaki is a chemical consultant for one of the large drug manufacturers of Osaka who were having a get-together of a number of their principal officers at Niigata in connection with a meeting of pharmacists of the prefecture, which was itself timed to coincide with [the] famous annual display of fireworks. It was part of their publicity program, quite in the tradition of the East, to arrange for several boats at great expense in which to entertain some of their principal customers. Yoshiaki & I and the Shimazonos were to have seats in the principal boat & as a result (or cause) I was asked to say a few words to the pharmacists convention after my lecture, interspersed among various papers & communications on the use of new drugs etc.

But in the morning we first drove down to the city where there was great excitement over the "Bon" festival, an annual Shinto affair (also participated in by Buddhists) and in connection with wh. I believe the fireworks were being held. A great procession was being formed in the streets with cars containing Japanese bands and singers and drawn by garlanded children. Huge bottles of sake mounted on carrying sticks each borne by 4 men were hurried through the streets and there was tremendous stirring and anticipation generally. We did not stop here long but went to see an old city garden belonging to the landlord's family of the day previous, all built in the Kyoto style with tea house, stone bridges, etc, but no actual water. The illusion of water, & it was a good one, was produced by a distribution of popple stones from a river bed & the little bridges.

After that we drove out in another direction from that taken the previous day to another smaller but somewhat older manor house. The manor itself had been in our host's family 900 years and the antiquity of the beautiful simple garden was shown by the towering cryptomeria trees. We were met & given fruit & tea by our host, a very old gentleman in yukata, and his beautiful wife. I was told later that the latter was a geisha from Niigata for whose sake he had divorced his previous wife. Since the war, & partly as a result of his family changes, his finances were much depleted. He was charming however, as was his wife, and after we had seen the house & garden and family chapel with its gilded memorial tablets going back to Kamakura times, we were given more refreshments before we started back. I wish I could give you the serene impression of that beautiful dignified open house, so cool and shady, surrounded by its garden glades, an asylum from the oppressive heat of the rice fields and open country.

Pictures give a poor impression of a Japanese house (I reflected the other day that the difference between a Western house and a Japanese house is that between a vertebrate and an arthropod: in the vertebrate, the skeleton — the halls & passages — is internal; in the arthropod it is external — the passages and galleries surround the rooms on the outside). As we drove off our host & hostess stood waving goodbye at the old gateway.

This time we were on time for lunch, which I had again in the rector's room & the lecture began at 1:00. I felt the second one went a little better. Towards the end of it some photographers came in & took some flashlight photos for the local paper. Afterwards we went down to the pharmaceutical meeting, where I gave my speech on the growing importance of fundamental science in modern biology & medicine & then we adjourned to the inn where Yoshiaki had transferred at the invitation of his associates from the drug co. There he & I and Shimazono shed our clothes for kimonos & thence, after putting on getas, we set out with Mrs. S in a car for the riverside. There we foregathered with a whole contingent of guests & officers of the drug Co & a great many geishas and many boxes of supper & bottles of beer & sake & went aboard the river boats.

The whole riverside was like a beehive & the number of boats packed in was tremendous. Some of the most interesting were the country boats, alive with old and young, many of which we had passed in the morning on our way along the river to the manor house as they came down the river to be ready for the great event. There was great discussion of who should be where in the boats. Yoshiaki & I & the Shimozonos were given the place of honor as strangers, & the old proprietress of the inn made a selection of the most desirable of her geishas to attend upon me as the foreigner of the party. And I must say that she picked out a very charming and attractive young creature of 18 in a pink kimono — all the girls in our boat had pink kimonos. I wish I could think of her name; it began with M.

We were all aboard by about 6:00. The boats moved into the stream about 6:30 or 6:45. The fireworks began at 8:00. In the meantime, we opened our lunchboxes, the wooden boxes well stocked with

rice & savories & fish and we were all plied with any amount of Jap. beer. There were some speeches & I had to make one, & M filled my glass as soon as it was empty and according to the custom I had to pass it to her by turns. By 8:00 the first rockets went up & from then on there was the most gorgeous & unstinted succession of bursting chrysanthemums of fire in the air and set pieces on the bank of the river that I have ever seen. There were two competing centres, one opposite us & one about a mile downstream. Japanese fireworks are really something to see. By the time they were underway, the beer & sake were having their effect on some of my shipmates but the girls knew exactly how to treat it all. I found myself with one on each side, M. on the right and another on the left, holding my two hands and exclaiming at each shower of flame. We got back to the inn about 11 or 11:30 & I recovered my Western clothes & walked home.

Next morning Yoshiaki & the Shimazonos & I were to start at 8:30 to catch the steamer for Sado Island.

I am not getting on with this letter as I should. It is like Tristram Shandy who took how many years (?) to cover the first 3 days of his life. I will post this as it is however. Farmy

Anne! I gave your address to a nice young Japanese girl of 18 today who was very anxious to write you. Her father has been most gracious to me. Do reply.

Sept 3, 1950   *Steamer to Sado Island*
                                           JW in Kyoto to Marblehead

Dear Anne & Jeff, I have a few minutes until I leave this little hotel & will carry on with my note in the meantime.

Sado Island, where Yoshiaki & the Shimazonos & I spent 2 nights, is a large, mountainous & very beautiful island about 20 mi across which lies off the West coast of Japan opposite Niigata. You will easily see it on the map. It is a three hours' trip to reach it at the nearest point by steamer, but one is never out of sight of land. Indeed, unless it is hazy, the blue mountains of Sado are plainly visible from Honshu. It is an out of the way district & certain parts of it are extremely isolated & have preserved many old ways of life. In Kamakura times

(12th & 13th centuries) one of the emperors was exiled there as a result of the efforts of an early shogun. Still earlier, I believe it was used as a place for prisoners who were sent there to work the gold mines. There is now a population of about 120,000 divided among several towns & many villages and scattered farms.

The steamer was quite crowded with people who included a trip to the island in the festivities of Bon, mostly from Niigata & its neighborhood. We got aboard at a quay about a mile up the river and it was interesting to watch the doings of the port as we steamed down to a breakwater marked with a red lighthouse. There were many of the Japanese fishing boats sculling in and out & just off the bar a whole flock of small handliners. It was a beautiful calm day for the crossing. We headed straight for the rocky shore of a small village where a boat with passengers was lying waiting for us. It seemed to me that we kept up speed to within a few yards of the rocks before we stopped. Then with a few strokes of their sculls, the boatmen laid their craft alongside & we exchanged passengers & proceeded to the main port where we were met by Drs. Kobayashi, Sano & another, all friends of Shimazono. They provided the hospital car & ambulance to transport us. No more now, for here comes the bus. Farmy

---

Sept 15, 1950   *Family visits, Sado Island*
                                     JW in Shingu to Marblehead

Dear Anne & Jeff, I posted my last letter just as I left Kyoto to go off on my walking trip with Kyoshi Kurahashi, but the letter only took me to Sado Island.

The contingent of doctors who met us at the dock drove us to the island hospital, which stands at a point not far from the centre of the place, & there we were served fruit & tea and shown about. It was my first visit to a Japanese hospital and I had never given any thought to the problem of the care of the patient. It will appear almost incredible to you that each patient brings his own servant or family to cook and look after him. The hospital provides kitchen space but no food although there is the beginning of a system of hospital meals. The professional nurses are therefore limited in their services to purely medical matters. As you walk through the passages & look into the rooms it is hard to distinguish the patient from his family or friends who have come to take care of him and who share his room. The typical Japanese bed is of course only a mat which is brought out and laid on the floor at night, so the problem of sleeping space is somewhat simplified. But in some cases western style beds were used for the sick. The confusion is really not as great as you might expect from this, and it must be reassuring to the patient to be surrounded by those he knows & cares for instead of the impersonal & often officious nurses we provide. There is great opposition to any change in this system such as is being agitated for by doctors of European & American training.

We were shown over the laboratories & X Ray room of the hospital & then taken off to lunch at a nearby inn by the two principal hosts, Dr. Sano & Dr. Kobayashi. The former had been a prisoner in Siberia for a number of years & had only recently been liberated. The latter was an obstetrician of about my age, who lived in the nearby town at the centre of the west coast of the island. He was our principal host, and his wife's family were all Sado people. He was a rather plump genial man, much according to my picture of an obstetrician, who would have dearly liked to live and work in Tokyo.

The inn was a large old fashioned Sado farm house, built about 3/4 century ago in the typical style of the island which I cannot easily describe except to say that there was a second story with a steep flight of steps like a ship's companionway stairs leading up to it. Part of the house, however, was open to the roof. We had a large & excellent meal and then, since I had expressed an interest in the old indigenous life of the island, we were driven off under the guidance of Dr. Kobayashi over a devious set of country lanes leading up into the hills where we were taken to an old farm belonging to a relative of Kobayashi's wife.

It was in the upper part of a green valley with a little river running down between terraced rice fields. Near the head of the valley & just above a Buddhist temple hidden in the woods, we found the house and farm buildings. There lived a family of 4 generations of intelligent, thrifty and prosperous people whose forebears had owned and cultivated the same fields — about 2 acres of them — for 300 years.

The present house, however, was only 130 years old. It was built much like the inn & its great beams, blackened with smoke (for no Japanese house has a chimney), were most venerable.

We all sat about in a circle in the "parlor" and were served fruit, cow's milk (the first I had been offered in Japan) & tea while we talked. The old grandfather of 80 and more had become a Christian in middle age, a rare & I should suppose somewhat courageous thing, and of course had brought up his family to be so. He was now too old to work and had turned the farm over to his son, of an age between 50 & 60, in the usual way. The latter had 3 sons, and of these the eldest was married to a charming looking girl who was the mother of 1 or 2 children. She was the only woman of the family who showed herself, and she was very shy. In the background we could see the old woman, bent almost double, hovering about in the kitchen.

Of the 3 sons, the eldest, who would inherit the place, worked on the farm when he was not acting as a teacher in a nearby school. The second, whom I talked most with, was home on vacation from the University of Sendai (I believe) where he was studying electrical engineering. He was a very bright boy and had hopes of visiting the U.S.A., as they all do. The youngest was sick & I did not see him. Altogether, they counted 3 active workers to till the 2 acres of rice paddies — rice is a highly intensive crop. I suppose this meant the middle aged father, his daughter-in-law and the eldest son, when school was not keeping, supplemented by others. The family also had some woodlands from which they cut. I was sorry to leave such an idyllic spot, where everything was so fresh & green in the warm sunlight of the later afternoon.

On the way home to Dr. K's town we were driven through another set of country lanes & past the scarcely discernible ruins of the old exiled emperor's palace, to a little hand pottery for making Sado ware. It was in the house of the owner who worked it with two apprentices. He was quite famous & in his younger days had made bronze figures but now, in his old age, he had turned to clay as an easier material. He greeted us in yukata and obi and his wife likewise in kimono. The apprentices wore white duck work clothes. They showed us the use of the wheel & we watched in fascination the different shaped pots grow as if by magic under the hands of the apprentice. I was asked to decorate several of them which I was told would be sent to me in Tokyo when fired. They only do the firing once in 2 months.

I was shown some of the old master's products and then given tea according to the tea ceremony. I bought a bowl, which you will see someday, & we drove off this time to the town on the shore where we were to stay. There were 4 of us off-islanders and it had been arranged that the Shimazonos should lodge with the Kobayashis & Miura and I with a brother-in-law who was a rich shopkeeper & merchant of the town. All our meals were to be provided by the Ks as hosts, at the latter's house.

We drove first, therefore, to the store which was really a general store or kind of primitive department store with the house at the back as usual. It was an astonishing revelation when we passed through the store and took off our shoes to enter a spacious and elegant house opening out upon a delightful garden containing a little pond & tiny foot bridge and closed off by a row of sheds at the back. Just beyond we could hear the noise of the sea against the beach. There were two large rooms surrounded by a gallery which were to be our living quarters for the 2 nights we were to spend there, and these were decorated with several quite valuable kakemonos and a bronze figure by our friend the potter.

Our host, the merchant, and his wife were much in the background since they were really lending their house and our primary host, Dr. K. The merchant's wife, I discovered, was a daughter of the old man of the farm we had visited earlier. We had a bath & I was given a specially large yukata made for the purpose by Dr. K's order since the ordinary ones are ludicrously short for me. Then, while supper was making, we went up to the roof to watch the sunset over the sea and the stormy clouds gather over the mountains under the force of a heavy on-shore wind.

Supper was cooked and supervised by Mrs K and turned out to be quite a banquet served on best china. According to true Japanese custom, we each ate off a separate little red lacquered tray or table about 18" x 12" & raised on legs about 8" from the floor. We were ordered in 2 opposite rows on the floor, quite formally, and the company consisted of Dr. K & the 4 of us. We were served by two daughters, one of Dr. K, the other the daughter of the merchant. Dr Sano was to have been there but came very late owing to a patient. He had some interesting accounts of his life in Siberia.

After supper I had quite a talk with Dr. K's son, 18 years old, who was very bright & much interested in English. The women folk, other than Mrs S, hovered in the background. There also appeared the merchant's younger brother (married & with children) whom, in default of a son, the merchant had adopted.

Next morning we all breakfasted together & then Miura & I went off to pay a visit to the high school where we had an interesting talk with the principal and visited several classes. Coeducation has recently been introduced but for the most part the classes were predominantly male or female. I was much impressed by the efficient way they were teaching English. The average student has a much better speaking command of it than most of ours do of French or German and, considering the difficulty that it must present to them, that is something to be proud of for them. The students all seemed very intent.

After that Yoshiaki & I & Motoko (K's daughter) & one of the children of the family went swimming & then, following lunch, Miura & I and the Shimazonos & Dr. K all set off in the hospital car to visit the main old town of the island where the mines as well as some potteries are located. On the way, over the tiny shore road, we passed some very primitive villages and at one we stopped to visit a house. As we were about to leave the place, we stepped down onto the beach to have a look at the fishermen busy about their nets & boats and there we ran into the head man of the fishermen's organization who turned out to be the husband of one of Dr K's patients. So he called some of his friends & they hauled down & launched their boat in order to take us for a spin. We were ashamed to cause so much trouble but they would not have it otherwise and, after taking on a supply of beer & dried cuttlefish, we set off and were steered out through the maze of ledges over which a low lazy groundswell was washing. The boat had a little outboard motor which failed us several times but finally got us home again.

I was interested to pass a deeply tanned fisherman swimming about among the ledges with a spear in his hand and a water glass strapped over his eyes. He was after [a fish called] tie and his fishing was all done underwater. It was fine to see him dive & disappear, like a loon, and wonder where he would next come up. He was a fine swimmer as you can imagine. This method of hand fishing is very common.

The potteries were larger & less interesting on the whole than the one we had seen the day before but I enjoyed a lesson at the wheel. We were tired when we got back and I was glad enough to relax in the bath & put on my big yukata before supper which was a feast as usual. Afterwards it had been arranged that a group of local dancers was to come and demonstrate the Sado Island miners' dance, which is one of the most famous old folk dances of Japan, and is known everywhere. Often it is done by moonlight on the beach. It is really a highly formalized representation of the labors of the miners, accompanied by singing and, as I recall, some simple instruments.

The performers were local townspeople who cultivated this dance particularly and seemed to form a kind of guild or club. They wore deep blue kimonos and a kind of straw head umbrella, folded [drawing], which was very decorative. The complicated dance was beautiful and they took it very seriously. There were 12 or 15 of the "professional" dancers and a number of guests. Since the dancers were slow in preparing, Mrs. S. entertained us meanwhile with the Japanese harp, which is not at all like our western harps but shaped like a great hollow tree trunk. I was glad to drop into bed at about 11:30 after it was all over & I had had a try at the dance under the direction of Matoko who kept laughing outright at my mistakes.

We were up early next morning to drive to the S.E. end of the island to catch a small boat which would take us to Honshu, far down the coast towards Kanazawa where we were going. The trip across that way was 6 or 7 hours but would save much rail travel. The drive along the bay & then over he hills and past the mountain farms looking out to sea, all in the fresh of the morning, was very nice and lasted 2 1/2 hours. But alas! when it was over we found that the boat had not come over owing to the rough water and that we should either have to wait 24 hours or go back on the steamer in the P.M. from the usual port.

We decided on the latter but, before starting, we got a boatman to take us out to a small nearby island and along the shore beyond. I was much struck by the ease and precision with wh. he handled his boat with his single clumsy-looking scull oar. The coast was like the hills and sea in a Chinese or Japanese painting. Terribly steep mountains and cliffs & caves at the water's edge — and the little islet was joined to the headland with a steeply-arched bridge under which we shot with a single stroke of the scull. There was a cottage on the islet and the whole effect, as we cleared the ledges over which the waves from the Japan sea were washing, was to make me feel I was living in the world of an old Nankin or Canton plate, miraculously brought to life and action.

About 1/2 mile beyond, along the steep coast with cliffs rising 100 ft or more, we were astonished at the sudden opening up of a deep narrow cove. It was one of the loveliest I have ever seen, with a sandy beach at the end and a couple of fishing boats drawn up in it. The banks were bold and wooded and on one side was a cave which the villagers used as a cool cellar for thir perishable goods. We went ashore for a few minutes and walked up through the woods & past 3 or 4 houses which made up the village. We paid a call & had some talk with the people of one house, who told us there were rice paddies on the high land back of the cliffs. Time was pressing so we hurried back to the boat & made a direct return to the waiting car which drove us back to the hospital. There we had a late lunch with our doctor friends & had just time to catch the steamer for Niigata.

The change of plans meant we should have to sit up all night in the train for Kanazawa where I was to give a lecture at 10 next morning. We had the ordeal of waiting from 11 to 2:30 A.M. in the station at a small place called Nagaoka but, when we arrived there, we found that the R.R. people at Niigata had told them of our coming & we were shown into the station master's room where some benches were put together so that we could lie down.

At Kanazawa we were met by Dr. Utai from the university & by the university secretary & also by the governor's representative and by a Civil Affairs man of the occupying forces — that is the effect of travelling in the provinces — & taken to a delightful little Japanese inn where breakfast was waiting for us. There was not much time to eat it & get on to the university where I paid a call on the rector before going to the lecture. Afterwards they gave us lunch & took us on to see the laboratories. At the end of the afternoon we went to a porcelain maker's where they produce the old Kutani ware characteristic of the district. Then home for a rest before going out to dine with the rector & one or two others.

He was waiting for us in yukata at an old-fashioned little inn high up on the hill in the park once part of the Daimyo's garden. It looked out through the trunks and tops of the big old trees toward the sunset and across to another hill & park where the old Maeda castle once stood until it was burned 90 years ago. (Only the gates & stone foundations now remain.) We were given a fancy dinner served by geishas who sat & fanned us and entertained us until it was time to go home. The old rector felt very genial as a result of all the sake we drank & I felt rather sleepy.

Next morning our hosts called for us to take us to the old palace, now public property and run as a museum but originally used by the daimyo's mother. It was in another part of the same park where we had dined the night before. The last Maeda to live there was the widow of the daimyo who had brought up Yoshiaki's mother-in-law. It was a huge house, full of treasures and beautiful things. Unfortunately the kitchens were taken down. We saw the little stage where the Noh dances were given. I was told that in old times the whole establishment had had 200 - 300 retainers to look after it. The custodian gave us the tea ceremony at the end of our visit.

Then, since I had expressed great interest in Noh, they had arranged with the Society which puts on the Noh plays to give us, not of course a full production, but one or two sample songs and dances at the Noh theater. Noh is the name for a very ancient form of dramatic dance and song, chiefly kept alive by the interest of sophisticated old people, mainly men, and often before the war under the patronage of the great. The old Maeda had been a great patron of Noh which had flourished in Kanazawa as a result. The players are usually business or professional men who are in a sense amateurs, but their standards are really professional. We were taken to a large Noh play house with a beautiful dance floor specially made to be springy and resonant, for the timed stamping of the dancers is a great element in the performance. We were greeted by a group of the players, of whom the principal one was a local pharmacist, and after tea the show began. I will not attempt to describe it but I will point out that the players wear fantastic masks & very beautiful old Japanese costumes.

After this exhibition we went to have a look at the ruins of the castle & then home to lunch. While we were finishing, we had a call [visit] from Prof. Hibino, who is a plant physiologist who had lived many years in Formosa. He took us walking in the surrounding hills in the afternoon and left us at the inn in time for supper.

Next morning we were up & off on the mountain R.R. leading to Nagoya via Gifu, where the cormorant fishing flourishes. Utai & Hibino were at the station to bid us farewell & presented us with a basket of fruit which came in very handy on the 11 hr trip. When asked what strikes me most about Japan, I can honestly answer "Japanese hospitality."

Nagoya is one of the great cities of Japan & its university is one of the 2 or 3 top ones. According to present plans, I shall spend a week or 10 days there in Nov., lecturing. Dean Sugawara of the Sci. Fac., whom I had met with Mizushima in Tokyo, and Kubo, the physical chemist, met us at the station as well as the Civil Affairs man. The former pair took us off to supper & then I went to my billet at the Bankers Club. Here Yoshiaki left me to go back to Tokyo.

Next day the university people showed me the city & their labs and arranged to take me down to the biological station belonging to the university near Toba on the following day. Kubo, Sugawara and the director of the station called for me at an early hour and we had a pleasant talk all the way to Ise, which is the oldest & proudest of the Shinto shrines of Japan and the Mecca of Shinto piety. It is directly connected with the emperor. We visited both the outer shrine and the inner one, which is some miles from it. In both the actual buildings are recent, for it has been the custom to rebuild them every few years, but the woods are primeval & have been sacred ground from prehistoric times. It was a beautiful day and the peace and beauty of these sacred groves, particularly those of the inner shrine with the River of Seven Bulls flowing through it, made a great impression.

As we passed one of the temple buildings I was lured by the faint noise of a flute from inside and started listening to the strange Eastern tune. My friends had a word with a priestess who said that, if we waited a little while, we might go in and see the sacred dance. It is called Okagura and is a form of the dance given in the imperial household as Gagaku. That we did. Kubo, who is very modern & indifferent to tradition, was rather scornful & sat cross legged to the disapproval of Sugawara, who sat in the usual kneeling position. The thing that impressed me most was the music — flutes & pipes, chanting & clapping of hands, also some drums (as I recall) & the costumes of the priestesses. They wore red silk trousers & white silk tunics and the trousers were much longer than their legs so that the effect as they walked was most curious, their feet being entirely inside [drawing showing trousers trailing on the floor].

After our stop at Ise we resumed our journey via Toba to the little island laboratory at Sugashima. We were met at the fishing town by a fine looking boatman who took us over to the island. The trip was much the same distance as that from Woods Hole to Hadley's and very fine. The island was quite mountainous, perhaps 1 1/2 or 3 mi long and 1/2 to 3/4 miles wide. Kubo & I went swimming and then sat watching the fishing fleet of hand liners come in before a leading wind & on the flood tide, sails white in the sun, while supper was making by the boatman & his wife & under direction of [Dean] Sugawara. It turned out to be quite a feast — two kinds of abalone, one raw, one boiled, gathered by the boatman's wife, who was counted one of the best divers of the island and looked the reputation, a wonderful sukiaki & other things.

Next morning we breakfasted long as we talked of Japanese life & customs vs those of the U.S. and then boarded the station boat to circumnavigate the rocky island & visit the lonely fishing village on the seaward side. So back to pick up our bags & go to the mainland where we caught the train. Sugawara insisted on going all the way to Kyoto with me (4 or 5 hrs,) as he admitted afterwards, largely for a chance to have a good talk of things in Japan & the affairs of the university. It turned out to be a most valuable talk for me & the time passed like a flash. On the way we lunched on cold rice & boiled abalone with the aid of chopsticks, at which I am now quite adept.

At Kyoto Dr Tanaka met us & I took him & S[ugawara] out to dine before going to my hotel. S stayed overnight & I saw more of him next day.

Still I am getting farther & farther in arrears in my chronicle. Here I am now in Osaka, with a host of adventures of 2 weeks behind me which I have yet to record. I am coming to regard these letters as a kind of diary of my doings — I keep no other — and I hope you will not destroy them. I shall get a batch of letters today at Civil Affairs & am hoping for news of home. I think of you all constantly but so far I have had only one letter (from ACW) from home. Give my love to all, especially Aunt Susan. I have had no moments for writing except what I find for these letters. Write soon.

Yr. devoted old Farmy

September 24, 1950 (postmarked Oct 3) *Mt. Fuji and Catching Up JW in Tokyo to Cambridge, Massachusetts*

Dear Anne & Jeff, Here I am back again in Tokyo with a huge backlog to tell you of. But I was most disappointed not to have any letters from either of you when I arrived. You must write and let me know what has happened. I have never heard from Jeff even once & from Anne only once. [Next is inserted:] Since I wrote this, a letter which was misplaced in Civil Affairs in Osaka from ACW has turned up. It was the second and tells of giving up yr. job [end of insert] but I believe I have managed to write you a good many pages in the midst of a fairly full schedule. I enclose some photos which were taken on the occasion of the fireworks at Niigata.

I am off to Hakone for the day & perhaps the night also, with Mizushima though I must be back tomorrow to see about some mimeographing for my lecture on Tuesday. He will be here soon, but I will make a start.

Dr. Tanaka gave me a very good time in Kyoto. Kyoshi [Kurahashi] was waiting for me there at his aunt's house when I arrived, ready for the walking trip & went with us about the city. I stayed however in the Myako Hotel where I was billeted by SCAP. Kyoto is a delightful contrast to Tokyo — full of ancient temples and palaces and with the most wonderful gardens. It was unhurt in the war (for which I believe we are largely indebted to Langdon Warner [of Harvard] who is held in great veneration there as a result. I wrote him so the other day) and it lies, full of green, in the lap of the hills.

I will not attempt to describe the temples and houses, not even the

great West Hongwanji temple with the wonderful screen & shoji and ceiling paintings from the old palace of Hideyoshi, nor the beautiful austere Katsura Palace of much the same era on the outskirts of the city. You know Kyoto was the home of the emperor from early times until 1868 — the Meiji restoration — when he came to Tokyo.

Here comes Mizushima.

Friday — I have not had a moment since Sunday. There are so many people to see & plans made for me that I have to get up very early in the morning to prepare my lectures. I have never been given so much attention in my life & Miura says he thinks it exceeds that given to any visiting scholar in Japan he has heard of. It is all due to a combination of circumstances. [Continues without a break.] Let me tell you of my recent doings.

The outing with Mizushima was very pleasant. He is two years older than I & a very strong little man. We got onto the train at Tokyo Central & at the next stop were joined by Dr. Bekku, who had been president of one of the big electrical companies of Japan until the "purge" after the war. He was a very nice man. Then at Yokohama three more of M's cronies got aboard. The most interesting was the ex Vice Admiral Baron Nawa (there are no more admirals or generals in Japan) who is the man who devised & developed the two-man submarine about which we heard so much during the war. He told me a good deal about it & how it took advantage of some of the special discharge properties of storage batteries. It went 25 knots for the first 25 miles & then at lessened speed for the next 50. He is a very able electrical and naval engineer but a most whimsical & witty man of aristocratic bearing & ancient family. Then there was a physicist & another.

At Odawara we changed cars and at Hakone got an ancient automobile which drove us up to the pass overlooking the mountain lake on one side & Mt. Fuji on the other, with a view of the sea in the distance in two directions — towards Atami in one way and the W. coast of the Izu Penninsula in the other. Fuji, which is as shy as any Japanese girl, was covered in clouds. We had lunch in the pass & then set off for a moderate walk over a long ridge. By & by, as the sun began to sink, the clouds over Fuji started to lift &, though she was never clear, we could soon see her top & portions of her flanks against the sunset.

She is 12,300 ft high & rising, as she does, from sea level with such perfect symmetry, she presents a wonderful sight.

[Ex-Admiral] Nawa had made arrangements for dinner & entertainment by geishas at an inn near Hakone & we were glad when we got there after dark. We all had a hot bath, put on yukatas & were soon busy about our food & sake. About 9 we drove off in another rickety car to catch the train at Odawara & I rolled into bed in Tokyo about midnight. I hope to see Nawa again & I believe I may do so this Sunday for I am going on another walk to Zushi, where he lives, with some other people.

On Monday I took some lecture material to the office to be mimeographed, took care of some letters & then had a call from Nitta, the X-Ray crystallographer from Osaka. After that I went to the dispensary to see about an itching in my eyes. I did not want to take any chances with trachoma after staying with the trachoma-infested Ainus in Hokkaido. And then to lunch at the Union [?] Club. In the P.M. I worked in the office on lectures & in the evening in my room.

Tuesday was the day of my first main lecture in Tokyo. I took a sandwich lunch from the snack bar at Empire House & armed with my mimeographed sheets to help the audience follow me, I drove to the university. I have a nice sunny office there also & as soon as I arrive tea is brought to me. Also I receive a string of callers which I am glad of. I had no sooner opened my door than some came in and stayed till lunchtime. About 20 of us gathered round a big table in M[izushima]'s room & ate our sandwiches while we talked.

A stream of people came in to greet me & the room was very crowded before the lecture, which was at 1:00. I had no time to collect my thoughts in consequence, but it was fairly successful. There were about 160 people & the room overflowed & there were not enough sheets to go round, but I believe they understood most of what I said. I know the sheets were a great help. Some of the medical faculty as well as those of science came. Afterwards, many came into a smaller room for a discussion. Then Mizushima & I drove off in the university car to see the Nezu Collection, which is the greatest private collection of art in Japan. M is an old family friend of Nezu's & had arranged for it. The present Nezu, who is president of the Nikko R.

Road, greeted us and gave us some green tea, cakes & fruit while several of the custodians or caretakers brought out one after another of the most superb paintings, beginning with the Ashikaga (Muromachi) period. We were also shown some very beautiful earthenware & porcelain, some Chinese & some Japanese. We only had time to see a tiny part of it & I have been invited to another visit next week.

After about 2 hrs of this we were sent home in Mr. N's dilapidated car & I took Mizushima & Nitta, who was waiting for me at the hotel, out to a very fancy dinner at a Jap restaurant. It cost me $18 but was delicious & no complaints.

The Nezu house stands in a very fine park or garden, or at least it did, but the house was burned during the war & there remain only the concrete storage houses. The collection is aired & gone over twice a year. But they will not open it during the wet summer months.

On Wednesday I was up at 5:45 to work on the materials of my next lecture (Thursday) & took it to the office to be mimeographed. Then I went back to pack my things and transfer to the Imperial Hotel which is more comfortable than the one to which I went on my return. It was designed after the great earthquake of 1923 by Frank Lloyd Wright & I am sure you have seen pictures of it. It is a remarkable building but rather dark & gloomy & the food is not much better than in any other of the occupied hotels. But as it is nominally reserved for generals, the service is excellent. I have a fairly large room with a huge luxurious bathroom & a lot of storage space for books & clothes. In the P.M., rather fed up as a result of moving, I took a nap & then went out to have a look at some of the paintings at the Ueno Museum (The Imperial Collection). One should see them every day for a little while for years to learn to understand their subtlety.

On Thursday I got up very early to work up more lecture sheets & then drove up to the university after working in my office at ESS in the A.M. I got there in time for lunch & several visits but had no chance to go over what I wanted to say & I felt very disappointed with the performance. The audience was about the same as at the previous lecture. Afterwards we had another discussion & after a few exchanges with various friends, I was whisked off by some of the younger members of the department including some from the Inst. of Science and

Technology at Komba to visit the Folk Museum & its director Dr. Yamaji, who is a friend of L. Warner & was once at the Fogg [Museum in Cambridge, Mass].

He gave us all a warm welcome & took us through his beautiful collection. It illustrates the wonderful way in which art adorned every phase & detail of life in medieval Japan. I was fascinated by the exquisite grass raincoats. One sees more ordinary ones in passing through the countryside — they make men look like birds — but these had exquisite ornamentation.

As I have exclaimed before, what a fusion of art, life and nature there was in old Japan! The pottery was of great beauty of shape & color. Y[amaji] ended by giving us green tea & Kanazawa rice cakes in his house & showing some fine things, a beautiful Sesshu kakemono being the best. I was astonished to see a Cezanne on his wall — a large unfinished oil — & to feel how well it seemed to fuse with the Japanese things. Yamaji has great taste & I felt much in common with him. We are to meet again & dine together & he is to tell me many things I want to know — places, people, just what is happening to the Japanese artistic tradition.

After this visit to a most sophisticated & cosmopolitan house, but with a warmth of real friendliness & enthusiasm, I hurried back to Miura's for a dinner party & to spend the night. I was late & the other guests were there. There were only two of them, a Japanese diplomat who had been minister to Sweden & elsewhere and the head of the Jap. cultural relations mission in Siam & his daughter, whose husband was killed in the war.

Yoshiaki had arranged this dinner party when I complained that I hardly saw any upper class Japanese women (that they are always evaporating) and because of the Siamese connection. The man says he will give me letters to people in Bangkok who can arrange things for me there as I would like. He was a most agreeable fellow who had lived many years in Paris & other parts of the world. Of course he spoke excellent English.

This morning I got up at 5:50 to do a little work until the two Miura children came into my room for entertainment. Then we all had breakfast & I went with Yoshiaki to give a talk at a girls' college where he gives lectures to supplement his income. It was very interesting to see the place & all the students. They arose & bowed low as we entered. I told them a little about American college life & they had many questions to ask. I think they are very diligent and never see any boys.

After that I went back to Miura's house to pick up some sandwiches & then we walked to the university where I had callers from the Inst. of Sci. & Tech. until lunch time. After lunch we had a big round-table conference and a good discussion of matters raised in my lectures. That was the most successful thing so far. And afterwards Mizushima took me to see a seal-maker who is going to make me a Japanese seal with my name in Japanese characters. He is the best in Tokyo & an artist at it. M had known him as a schoolboy. He had made 4 designs of which I chose one. He lives of course over his shop in the old Edo manner and we were taken up to his living room, in pure Japanese style with a tokonoma containing some treasures & flowers, where we were served tea, cakes & fruit and had a good talk about the tradition of art expressed in the life and everyday utensils of Japan & the waning of a great tradition.

We men sat cross legged while the wife & daughter appeared and reappeared with tea and sat kneeling in one corner of the room as we talked. He gave me a demonstration of his craft, very simple & very beautiful. I enclose his design for my seal & his name and address which he wrote for me with a brush in an exquisite hand. Writing is a fine art in Japan and the supreme beauty of their brush work in painting, which is not approached in any western picture, is a consequence of this.

My great lament is the loss of the old traditions by the Japanese in their pursuit of our shoddy ways: Our standard of living has become so high that we cannot afford anything of real beauty! The stamp maker brought this out very clearly; so did the umbrella maker in Gojo of whom I will write later. In my opinion it is closely connected with the loss of respect and reverence and a sense of religion, and the corresponding growth of casualness, individualism and egoism which is spreading from the West. Certain absurd material comforts like bathrooms, effortless transportation by wheels, overheated rooms, food available without any effort at a minute's notice, shows which we can take in passively without the need of understanding or imagination — these have become values to us which have displaced a great tradition within which and because of which, individuals are really much more free and able to express themselves and work out their own genius at whatever level than with the facilities of an industrial age. That kind of tradition leads to real beauty in all lines of work from the top to the bottom.

We had much of this in the West long ago at a time when the arts flourished as they do not any longer. Perhaps the reason why the great contribution of our Western Age, modern science, is so successful is because it, like the art of the past, is based on a consistent, steadily developing tradition, and on the discipline of those brought up in it. Scientists have to work in the tradition. [sentence inserted] We in the West (e.g. Conant & many others who speak of the social function of Art & Science and the relevance of Knowledge) think of human enterprises as justified by their effect on the material life of the community. Actually, as the East well knows, nothing could be farther from the truth.

All efforts are valuable as they contribute to life as it culminates in Art and religion — life which expresses itself in the great creations of mind and spirit. Science, painting, music are such. It is true that they must be part of life, as I believe they have been in the East, where they have permeated in a subtle way [phrase inserted] all activities above the lowest, but they are the summit. That is all I mean by religion, for I have no theological beliefs as you know. I do not understand the more formal religion of Japan, of course, but I suspect it may represent, as in Shintoism, a kind of ritualistic realization of life in the tradition of beauty, and the conventions of a society in which everything is appropriately adorned in a way that makes it religious — rather than a matter of every day morals and theology like ours. I think there was very high morality in Japan where the religious tradition as I have tried to interpret it touched everything.

What a terrible effect the Scientific Age has had on life. I believe that in almost every respect except the philosophical one it has cheapened and lessened and confused life. Science is valuable because of the wonderful philosophical picture it has given us, as in biology and physics and mathematics. It has made us conceptually richer and, in that role, it belongs with the arts and is the primary adornment of modern life. But because of its material effects, it has been a source of evil and disintegration. The paradox is that we seem not to be able to separate the two sides of it, and it is certain that pure science could never develop without applied science and technology. We could never have developed the modern theory of the atom without the experiments that depend on modern electric power plants. The same is true of the pictures [sic] reached in astronomy and biology.

By wanting too much, we may lose the whole.

I love the old Japan, which I seek in every out-of-the-way corner of these islands, because it had that wonderful unity of a life permeated by a sense of beauty and "religion."

I have written too much & incoherently but I feel very strongly. Today is Saturday and I am going with Kyosan to see an exhibition of paintings by Sesshu & then later to his house this evening where a number of us are to read Macbeth. [Kurahashi remembers it as Hamlet, with him reading the part of Ophelia.]

Farmy

I shall have to fill in a tremendous gap in my next letter! I post this Sunday as I start for a long day in the country, walking from Kamakura to Zushi with some friends.

Oct 5, 1950 (postmarked Oct 31)   *Rickshaws and a Centrifuge*
JW in Kyoto to Cambridge, Massachusetts

Dear Anne & Jeff, I last wrote you Sat, nearly a week ago. I had a nice day with Kyosan [Kyoshi Kurahashi] at the exhibition of Sesshu paintings at Ueno & then in the evening at his house. Sesshu is I suppose the greatest of Japanese painters & was a contemporary of Leonardo da Vinci (about) or somewhat earlier. He lived in what is called the Muromachi or Ashikaga period, following the Kamakura Shogunate. He was a pupil of Sheebun & the whole school represented an innovation & an abandonment of the old Yamatoe style of painting & the colored Buddhist paintings of the Kamakura era. Their method was a development of the black & white paintings of the great Sung period of China of several hundred years before (and not of the contemporary Ming school, much inferior). Sesshu, who came from near

Hiroshima, went to China to study. He says he found no teacher but learned from the Chinese masterpieces & from the landscapes he saw. (But Japan on the shores of the Inland Sea near where he lived is equal to anything in China I am sure.) Most of his pictures were painted from his head but a few were done in the presence of nature. There is a wonderful freedom in his brush work and an almost brutal angularity of some of the strokes. The work is less minute than that of the Chinese masters. Perhaps the great popularity of Van Gogh in Japan may be related to a certain similarity I fancy I can see between him and Sesshu. In some of his pictures there is a trace of color but in my opinion the finest & most beautiful are black & white. They are on paper, not silk. And paper is the more durable.

In the evening I went to supper at Kyosan's house. At table were his older brother, a well-known actor, and a theatrical producer. His younger brother came in later. We had a delicious meal served by his mother (who did not sit down) & afterwards read Hamlet. The actor was very fine in voice and intonation, I got home around midnight.

Next day, Sunday, Miura & I & Mizushima went down to Kamakura for the day. We lunched with Mizushima's parents-in-law, an old fashioned couple about 80 years old, in their villa. Old Shoda, the husband, is the flour magnate of Japan & has introduced modern flour-milling machinery. He is, I suppose, very rich & his villa is the only one I have seen which is kept up in prewar style. The garden was in perfect order, our meal was served by several servants &, when I left, a rickshaw man took me down to the shore for the sake of a ride in a gentleman's private rickshaw. The narrow lanes of Kamakura with their hedges and basketwork fences are very charming — fortunately too narrow for cars.

The three of us walked over the hill to Zushi, another town of villas. On the way we had a fine view of the bold coast bathed in autumn sun. In the later afternoon the path dropped down to the long sandy beach of Zushi, backed by villas of the rich, and we walked along it to the house of old Mrs. Fujise & her son & his family. It was a luxurious villa with garden but no view. We were entertained with fruit, tea & cakes & had a nice talk. I had dined with the older son in Sendai and made a trip with him to Matsushima. The daughter of this family was about yr. age & a most charming person. When we left she walked along the beach with us to the tennis court where her aunt & uncle were playing. Just as dark was falling we caught a crowded train (the crowding on nearly all Jap. trains surpasses the experience of any Westerner) & got home in time for bed. (Reiko & the Miura children had gone down by train with us but had continued straight on to Zushi & joined us there at the Fujise house.)

The next day, Monday, is a blank for I forgot to make any entry in my pocket diary & I can't seem to recapture — No! Now I remember. In the A.M. I had a long call [visit] from Dean Sugawara of Nagoya University where I shall visit in early November. We talked of plans for my lectures, of Jap. life & custom, of SCAP & so on. He has made arrangements for the Jap. scientific magazine corresponding to the English "Nature" to publish one of my lectures complete in Japanese. Prof Egami will translate it. Sugawara is the one who took me to Ise & Sugashima, of which I wrote. He is a very fine man, about 2 years older than I & is one of a set of boon companions & old schoolmates (including Nitta, the famous crystallographer & crystal chemist of Osaka) of Mizushima & others. He is a very simple man but appears to be the embodiment of the hospitality & integrity of old Japan, aristocratic, public spirited, quite out of the current of modern Westernized life. His great-grandfather was the principal minister of the old Daimyo of Odawa at the time of the Meiji troubles and led the attack on the Satsuma forces when they came across the Hakone mountains. He was defeated but, after the fall of the Shogunate, his reputation was high & he was asked to go to Edo (Tokyo) & join the new govt. He refused because he thought it was contrary to his feudal duties. Sugawara's remote ancestor was minister of the Left at the court of one of the ancient emperors but [was] driven from favor by court intrigue, as I believe I wrote you once. It takes me back to the Tale of Genji.

After Sugawara left there was just time for lunch & I went to my nice sunny room at the university. I have two offices in Tokyo, my one at G.H.Q. in Empire House and that at the Imperial University. When I go to the latter so many people come in that there is no time to do any writing or thinking, but I like it. Then I walked over to the Miuras' house & Yoshiaki & Reiko took me down to the Ginza — the main shopping street of Tokyo — where I wanted to buy a wedding present for Reiko's sister. But the shops were closed. Then I suggested that we take the children to see the Am. film "Snow White" which was playing at one of the big movie theaters. So the parents went back to get the children and I stopped at my hotel for a bite to eat. The evening was quite a success & I was much interested in the reaction of the Japanese audience to our movie. Of course they see a lot of them & they & the radios are one of the most insidious forms of the horrible process of Westernization — far more potent than any planned propaganda of G.H.Q.

Next day, the 3rd, I gave another of my lectures, on heme proteins, which I believe went very well. The audience has stayed constant or increased somewhat during the series, which is most gratifying — about 160-175 I suppose. After the lecture, Mizushima drove me off to see the grounds of the Imperial Palace. He is a kind of tutor or lecturer in science to the imperial princes and so has the entree. It was a heavenly autumn afternoon and everything looked its best. To stand under the old pine trees on the beetling verge of the stone ramparts & gaze out over the great inner moat to the busy city beyond gave a feeling of peace & detachment. We also drove past the great sunken valley or garden, excavated by hand several centuries ago, overhung by trees. And we visited the greenhouses and gardens where they train up the tamed dwarf pine trees. There used to be 6000 retainers to keep the palace & grounds in order; now there are only 1000 & it is, I am sorry to say, rather slovenly. We went to see the imperial music school where the tradition of the ancient Shinto music & the imperial Bugaku dances is kept up. Who should appear there (by chance) but Kurada, the master of ceremonies, who was most cordial. He invited me to come & beat upon one of the great Shinto drums, about 8 feet tall, which gave out a most venerable noise, & he promised to send me any number of tickets to the performance of the imperial Bugaku dance on the following Saturday. (Next day 5 tickets were delivered at the hotel.) Then we went to the stables which I had seen before & where I met the master of the court riding school. He asked me if I would like to join it, but of course I have no time for such things.

In the evening the Miuras & I were giving a dinner jointly at their house for a number of university people & I went directly there from the palace. Japanese food & European wine.

The next day to the univ. in the A.M. where as usual I had a sand-wich lunch with the crowd & then afterwards I drove off to the Institute of Science & Technology at Nokayama [Komba?] to attend a meeting of the committee on the Ultra-Centrifuge which they are now building in Japan. I felt very much pleased to be asked to take part in their deliberations. The instrument is really complete but they are having a good many troubles with it. The high grade alloy steel is not what it should be and several of the rotors have exploded under the terrific stresses set up. Then too they fail to get good definition in their photographs of the moving boundaries. I was able to make one or two suggestions of possible tests, but I am really wholly ignorant of the practical side of such things. The instrument was beautifully machined & very impressive as they ran it for us. We had a good tea & talk & I went home by train with Dr. Watanabe, who came to the hotel for a nice visit before dinner. He is one of the chief promoters of the centrifuge.

That evening I gave a small dinner party at the Union Club for Matsudaira [grand master of ceremonies], Kurada [master of cere-monies] & Col. Bunker [aide-de-camp to MacArthur.] The last was very late due to the caprices of his boss who he says keeps frightful hours. We had some good French claret & rather tough beef steak but it was pleasant. I told Kurada I was anxious to meet the Indian minis-ter to hear about India & perhaps get an introduction to Nehru (for I have a great admiration for him & wish to hear his opinion about this Western shroud that seems to be threatening the East from both sides, U.S.A. & U.S.S.R.) Kurada offered to escort me himself to a cocktail party next P.M. to meet Mr. Chettur, the minister in question.

Next day I went to the lab as usual & gave my lecture in P.M. I was to have gone for a second visit to the Nezu Collection but it was rainy so of course they would not open things & I went to the seal maker instead, of whom I believe I wrote you. At about 6:15 Kurada called for me and I went to the cocktail party where I met Chettur & his wife. She was a small dark woman in Indian dress with many jew-els. In particular she had the most magnificent earrings of pearls & rubies, which she wore again when I dined with her later. Chettur was tall, imposing & very dark. They are from the Madras region. I had a good talk with Chettur about the East & the West & he invited me to dinner. He is an extremely intelligent & quite anti-West man. I sympathize with India in her attitude of aloofness in this struggle between the so-called Western democracies and the so-called Communists. But whether she can remain free of attachments with either side, I wonder. I hope so. I also met several interesting people from China — China traders have been forced to leave. One was the representative of a Danish shipping co. He had been interned by the Chinese Communists for nearly a year but he admitted that the present absence of corruption among the officials was a most extraordinary change.

Next morning Kyoshi's older brother, Takeshi, took me to see the museum collection relating to Jap. drama at Waseda University, where he teaches. They have a wonderful collection of Ukiyoe (block prints) of Jap. actors — about 50,000. I had lunch with Dr. Bekku & a conference on heme proteins in the P.M. In the evening I was taken to a tremendous dinner with geishas by Mizushima's uncle, Dr. Shoda at a Japanese club. Shoda is the president of a yeast company, corresponding to our Fleischmann's, & wanted a letter of introduction to some biochemist in U.S.A. interested in fermentation & yeast problems for the head of his research group who is going to U.S.A. This was a perfectly reasonable thing & I was glad to give him a letter to my old colleague T.B. Stair, now at Univ of Indiana. But of course there was no need of such a banquet to justify my letter. That is typically Eastern. We had much sake and the madame of the restaurant played the Japanese harp for us. She had once been in the U.S.A. at Hollywood & once played to Hoover in the White House. I am fortunately much more resistant to sake than most Japanese. I was presented with a roll of very beautiful pre-war brocade by the principal geisha (actually of course, it was from the host) for my daughter & in due time, when I come home, you will have it, Anne.

Next day I met Kyoshi, my devoted walking companion, at 8:30 at Tokyo Central Sta. with my knapsack & we took the train for Numazu on the coast near the foot of Fuji. We were there by noon & had just time to catch a small steamer running down the W. side of the Izu Penninsula. We left her at Hedda, a small primitive village at the head of a deep bay in the precipitous penninsula & made haste up the mountain. Everywhere we went the great snow-covered Fuji was looking at us — sometimes uninterrupted over the great expanse of water between us and Numazu; sometimes partly screened by the trees & autumn grasses; sometimes half hidden by a ridge or the shoulder of a lesser peak. She is like a guardian spirit, from whom there is no hiding and who is always ready to set you right when your sense of devotion fails. It was cold on the summit of our local peak & nearly sunset as we reached the top.

Just as we started down, the great red disc made contact with the Western hills 30 or 40 miles away over the Gulf. Then the stature of Fuji seemed to grow. We had a long walk down to our inn at Shuzenji in the dark & we got there, very cold, in the middle of the evening. I was shivering cold and so, I think, was Kyoshi but a good soak in the hot spring bath soon made up our debt of heat and we put on warm doteras (quilted robes) furnished by the inn & took our supper cross legged. We had walked 6 hrs. & were hungry. So we slept well until soon after dawn, though there was much noise from other guests of which I was dimly aware.

Next day we got a country bus — very rough — which took us well down the centre of the penninsula. There we got off & had a delightful walk over foot paths to the East coast, emerging just S of the great mountain of the penninsula without having time to go up it. Our walk lasted 7 hrs. A young Japanese mechanic from near Numazu attached himself to us this day. He hardly spoke but was glad of our company & our maps. He would never have got there otherwise. As we crossed the height of the land we could see water on 3 sides & the volcanic island of Oshima out to sea & looking very large & near. We ate our lunch of cold rice on the top. We lost our way somewhat in going down, which involved an hour's extra walking but arrived at dusk at a little village on the coast. Coming out upon human activity & rice fields & thatched farm houses in the late afternoon, in the chilly air, was delightful. No one has more dignity than a peasant carrying a heavy load as you pass him (or her) on the path. The reserved formality of the greeting, the sense of his own proud independence in pursuit of his goal, and the fellow feeling which you have for him as another traveler sharing the common experience of the road — give meaning to the encounter which no other passing has. What a loss it was when walking ceased to be the principal mode of travel. Only riding, perhaps travel by sail or paddle, can approach it. And the sense of parting, as you say good bye and turn down the path, so far exceeds that on being rolled away on wheels like a fat pig being carried to the slaughter house!

We had a long trek back to Tokyo, partly by bus & partly by train (over 4 hrs) but arrived very happy after the weekend.

Next day (Monday) Dr. Oka, a theoretical physicist of the Kobayashi Institute called for me at 9 to take me out to his institute. He brought his wife & 5 year old son, the former in kimono & bearing a present of autumn apples, for the sake of the drive in my shining G.H.Q. sedan. The little boy had, I believe, never been in a car before. We dropped him & his mother at the boy's kindergarten on our way. We had a nice talk at the institute about science & philosophy & what was going on there &, after a sandwich lunch with the staff, I was taken back to the house of the director, on the way to Tokyo, to see his magnificent collection of swords — a really great collection, some of them very old. No hand must be allowed to touch the blade. Twice a year they are wiped with a special powder but otherwise only with a silk cloth. The value attaches to the steel, not to the handles & mounting which are the showy part. And so home to a supper by myself.

No more now. I am at present in Kyoto & shall soon go to Nagoya, then Osaka, then Tokoshima & then for a two weeks' walk through the fastnesses of S. Shikoku with Kyoshi on my way to Kyushu.   Farmy

---

October 6, 1950 (postmarked Oct 20)   *Typhoon at Nara*
                                                  JW in Shingu to Cambridge, MA

Dear Anne & Jeff, I am starting this account of my doings after I left Kyoto in the early part of Sept. As I told you, Kurahashi had come on from Tokyo (300 mi) to join me on a walking trip & we had been seeing Kyoto under the guidance of Dr. Tanaka there. It was one of his friends who gave us the grand tea ceremony, lasting 2 1/2 hrs, where I met the girl who was to write you — an extremely nice girl, daughter of Tanaka. Tanaka had also shown us some old handcraft work-shops, eg one where they make cloisonne; a place where they do hand weaving of silk brocades, using their long fingernails, which they file to obtain saw tooth edges for dealing with the threads; a dye works where they make wonderful stencil prints by ancient & complicated processes, washing them as the final step in the nearby river.

On Sunday morning we were to go up to Nara to see the temples and other antiquities of the 7th & 8th centuries & then Kyosan (that is his nickname) & I were to start on our travels over the mountains. The plan was for Tanaka & his son & K & me to meet at a stated time. When I got up it was raining furiously and blowing & I realized that the approaching typhoon, of which we had been told, was in the off-ing. By the time I had finished breakfast it was blowing very hard and the wind was whipping the branches of the trees of the hotel garden furiously. The ducks in the pond sat unhappily with their heads sunk upon their breasts. On the way to the station I saw many people buf-feted by the wind, their umbrellas wrecked. But still it was only a moderate gale.

The others were at the station & we boarded the train without getting wet. We got off at a way station to see an old pagoda & I must say got pretty wet, sharing an umbrella on the way to it. But the storm seemed to be moderating at that time. After seeing the pagoda we went back to the station & caught another train for Nara, where we arrived about lunch time. It was raining so hard then that we decided to indulge ourselves by hiring one of the charcoal-burning taxis, somewhat old & decrepit. And after a lunch of salt fish and Japanese macaroni, we set out in it, going first to the great Shinto shrine on the hillside in a primeval grove of venerable cedar trees of enormous age. This is a shrine associated with the Fujiwara family of Nara times, represented today by Prince Kondye.

Nara is a park-like city, rich in temples, many of which stand on forested mountain slopes. Our drive took us through the deer park, full of tame deer which are never shot and which form the forest pop-ulation of the sacred grove. At this time the rain came down in tor-rents and the wind was rising more & more. The road was strewn with smaller branches of the great trees, much as I remembered the time of our own hurricane [in 1938] and it was clear that the typhoon

was at hand. But we drove on & left our car at the red gate of the shrine. As soon as we entered the courtyard we saw a freshly uprooted cedar, one of the fine old trees, which had crashed over on a part of the shrine & crushed it. A priest came hurrying by to look at the damage. We walked back to the gate just in time to see a huge branch from the tallest of the great trees ripped off and fall near the gate.

It was time to go and we started down a path towards the car but we soon turned back again at the sight of the swaying branches and took shelter once more under the gate. But the big tree was menacing us and we hesitated to stay. So we ran down our path once more and gained the car. Not long afterwards, we heard later, the big tree fell on the gate where we had been standing and flattened it to the ground. We drove on in the car to another holy building on the hillside, this time a Buddhist temple filled with many ancient statues, some of them fierce-looking temple guardians, like demon warriors. It was a wild scene there and most exhilarating. All the wild spirits of ancient Japan seemed to be revived and the banging and slatting of everything, particularly some of the metal plates & inscriptions hanging from walls, pillars & ceiling, made a great racket. It seemed as if all the carved warriors had come alive. The savageness of it all is something I shall never forget & we were all awed by it. The priests had thrown open certain of the shutters for us, notwithstanding the wind, & I was afraid some of the statues would be blown over. Such wildness ill accords with the traditional peace of Buddha but goes well with the fierce warlike character of some of the minor tributaries.

The typhoon was now at the height of its frenzy and, as we drove off, it was a question how we could get down out of the wooded hillsides. The first way led us past many fallen & swaying trees and finally, after passing a man who beckoned frantically, we found ourselves in a cul-de-sac. But the driver managed to turn the car and we tried another way. This took us down a narrow road & past a little collection of houses in the woods. A man stepped out to speak to us for a moment and then we drove on. But a moment later we were stopped by a fallen tree just ahead. I was reaching for the handle of the door to get out and clear the way, when there was a terrific crash & a huge pine, perhaps 120 ft tall, fell across the front of the car. It completely smashed the radiator & engine but, by a miracle, none of us were hurt. One of the branches bent in the roof of the main part of the car so that it touched our heads. The top of the tree smashed through one of the houses behind us & this may have somewhat broken its fall. But it was a close enough call.

We all jumped out of the car & the villagers came swarming from their houses, congratulating us in an awed manner. Other trees were swaying & bending & we stood in a sheltered space until the wind began to abate. It gave me a wonderful sense of elation & wildness which I am grateful for, and I believe brought out a side of Nara which is generally missed — Nara surrounded by the wars and furies of the fierce side of ancient Japan.

Later we walked back to the centre of town. There was of course no power or light & there was no running water in the little Japanese hotel where Kyosan & I put up. Tanaka & his son finally got a steam train back to Kyoto at 11 pm. We were bothered that night by rats in our room, the only time it has happened to me. It is a horrid feeling to be sleeping on your futon on the floor & have a big rat go scampering past. So we ordered a big mosquito netting to be put over us as a protection & slept better afterwards.

Next day was clear & bright, as is usual after a typhoon, but things were much disorganized. However we managed to get a steam train to Horyuji, the most ancient Buddhist centre of Japan, dating from the 7th & 8th centuries (the Asuka period.) It is only an hour from Nara. After a 40 minutes' walk from the station we reached the peaceful temple surrounded by a little village. It was hard to believe that once the level rice fields were the site of a big city, the ancient capital. There was a terrible fire in the temple about a year ago, which destroyed the frescoes in the main pagoda but all the priceless statues were saved. The main buildings have now been dismantled & are being put together again but the contents are on display in one of the other structures. The greatest thing, & certainly one of the great statues of the world, is a wooden standing Buddha, quite formalized but with a serenity and delicacy beyond description. Another close rival is a bronze sitting figure with face resting on the hand which is in a nunnery nearby. An obese and ancient man, hair cropped short, devoid of all attributes of either sex, with pale wrinkled face, opened the sanctuary for us at Kyosan's call, "Gomen kudasai" and sat impassively kneeling while we tried to take it in.

About lunch time we got back to the station & with much trouble made our way to Yoshino, where we wanted to start up into the mountains. Y is a small hill town, famous for its cherry blossoms in the spring, and the takeoff point for the priests, novices & lay members of a special sect of Buddhists who worship god as embodied in mountains & nature. There are various objects of worship for them in Japan and one of the most venerable is Mt. Omine which has been a sacred mountain for time out of mind. It lies about 30 kilometers (say 15 miles) from Yoshino at the end of a rough steep path. No woman has ever been there or is allowed to go, for it would distract the thoughts of the pilgrims.

We had been told it would be impossible to go up the mountain after the typhoon & I own it did seem uncertain, but we were burning with eagerness & impatience to try so we stopped to make some inquiries at an inn. There we were answered by the most unchecked flow of words from the hostess — a very nice woman — you ever heard. Of course I could understand hardly a syllable so I listened with impatience & incredulity & let my eyes take in my surroundings & the two handsome daughters, one with a baby. It seems the woman was telling as how it was impossible to get up the mountain because of landslides & washouts which made the path dangerous & impassable. But we were obstinate & finally she agreed that, since our hearts were set on it, she would find us a guide.

It was getting late — it was already after 3 — and we knew we could not get to the top that night (though under ordinary circumstances the priests often climb by night in order to be on hand for the miracle of the dawn). But there was a shelter halfway up where lived a monk & where we could stop. We laid in some food & a flashlight & some straw sandals for Kyosan, who had leather shoes, & finally were off & away sometime after half past 3:00. It was a fine path, often through tremendous cedars, though at times through smaller ones or clearings where there had been cutting. The brilliant afternoon sun & the distant views over the mountains & valleys & villages made us happy.

About an hour after our start we met our first contingent of priests coming down. They had gone up, I suppose, before the storm but might have gone up from another side. Their approach was known to us, before they came into view, by the ringing of their pilgrim bells. They were dressed in white, carried staves in their hands, had tiny openwork hats strapped to their head, wore heavy rosaries around their necks and, in addition, a big conch shell for a horn & on their bare feet were rough straw sandals. Their leader had a purple skirt. They were a fine sight as they came swinging down the mountain at a fast clip. They stopped for words with us and one, at my desire, stopped to blow his conch for us. Then we parted & continued our laborious ascent. Kyosan & I took turns carrying one knapsack & the guide carried the other.

Soon the sun set gloriously & we had to walk in the dark. Our guide said that every year several priests were killed by walking in the dark & falling off the edge but we had flashlights. It seemed a long way to our stopping point & we were glad at last to see the gleam from the house. The monk & his understudy were already asleep but it did not take him long to wake up. They built up a fire to make tea & we used it to toast some of the curious doughnut-like bread we had bought in Yoshino. This they supplemented by some of their own simple fare. They said I was the first foreigner to come and naturally they were excited. They shared their bedding with us (it was wet from the typhoon) and we all lay down to sleep in the faint light of the hanging lamp. I was a little cool & Kyosan, who feels the cold easily, was more so but we slept well, or at least I did, & awoke at dawn, in time to see the sun rise.

The monk had risen before us and had a fire going for tea & soup (I have forgotten whether we had rice or not) & after a good breakfast we were on our way. From here on the path was steep & we came to three landslides which were unpleasant to pass. I do not think we could have faced them in the dark. But otherwise the path was well worn by many pious feet. In places there were steps cut out of the rocks and here & there chains for handholds. Before noon we were within sight of the top where there was a temple & some lodgings, somewhat battered by the typhoon, for the pilgrims. At one place we came upon a breathtaking overhanging cliff where there was a length of dangling chain on which the pious would be lowered over the abyss to think upon their sins. At the top we lunched on some of our own food supplemented by tea & then sent back our guide, for we had decided to stay overnight. The original plan of following on over the mountains several days more was impossible due to the typhoon & lack of any guide who would undertake it.

The priests at the temple were friendly in showing us about & we were taken to some of the steep pinnacles & cliffs. The afternoon we spent sketching & sunbathing & drinking in the expanse of mountains & clouds. At night it was cold and at supper we were glad enough to crouch over the little earthenware firepot (hibachi) with a few lumps of glowing charcoal. After supper we went out to see the end of the day & the gathering clouds & darkness of night from the top of the mountain. In the morning, too, we were up & out before full daylight to watch the sunrise. How different the two are — sunrise & sunset — neither is anything like the other with reversed direction. That is partly the effect of physical causes, like the temperature distribution, but it reflects a much deeper difference coming from the whole set of our minds at the two ends of the day as well.

Soon after breakfast we were on our way down and began to meet groups of pilgrims swarming upwards. They were of all ages and always chose the hardest way, deliberately going over pinnacles & along knife-edge ridges. I can understand their religion better than most. What can be holier than a mountain or a waterfall? Where can we be closer to the centre of being than in the midst of nature? What purification of body & soul can equal that of a long perilous climb which takes us into the very essence of beauty? The panorama of nature at full intensity gives an exaltation of spirit that is a truly religious experience, though it can come only to the religious man, and it is kin to the experience of other values. Much of great Oriental art seems to be the expression of this. I suspect that the underlying concept of Eastern religion, as the contemplation of real meanings & values, is the right one. Of course it presupposes things to contemplate other than natural phenomena, eg human life & efforts, but it is the highest form of activity.

In its more passive phase it is represented by the religion of the mystic but in its active phase it leads to the ritualistic ceremonial religion with music & dance, and to art, and to science, too (as an active response of an intellectual kind to the object of contemplation). The idea of religion as a moral, social form of activity in daily life seems to me wholly secondary. I believe there was much rightness (though he did not mean it as I would) in old Vanderbilt's famous remark, "the public be damned." The real values have nothing to do with the public & the contemplation & service of them is the highest thing we can do. Indirectly, of course, the public gains from it. But the values of the public are nothing. And the religion of what I call "the rock-climbing priests" seems to me to be a very obvious and a particularly appealing expression of Oriental religion.

We reached our night's resting place about noon and lunched there as with old friends & then went on. We had crossed the land slips and felt better. About 2:20 after passing many pilgrims, we came upon our guide. He was concerned about us & had come up to meet us. He insisted on taking our pack & guided us down to the inn whence we had come. The old woman was more voluble than ever and prepared us a good meal while we washed and shaved preparatory to a long uncomfortable night in the train going cross-lots down to Shingu on the Kii Peninsula. The guide & his friend sat and talked to us while we ate and, when it was time to go, escorted us to the train at Yoshino.

Owing to the storm the trains had to be rerouted and this involved a stopover of 3 hours at a small country town called Gojo lying along a slowly flowing river. We were a little tired from our trip but spent our time strolling out along the banks of the river in the gentleness of the evening to an ancient temple. We passed many quiet farms along the river road, and children bathing, and fishermen. As we returned it was nearly dark with only the last colors of the West showing in the sky and in the river. By the time we got back to the town itself, it was quite dark and the houses were all lighted up. We had many glimpses of family life through the half-open shoji. And here we met the blind masseur, blowing his bamboo flute to give notice of his coming. It is the profession of the blind.

It was here also that we visited the umbrella maker of whom I spoke once before. He was in his shop finishing off some odds & ends with his family. I asked him about all the details of his beautiful craft and the time it took to make his products and the different kinds of umbrellas. He was pleased indeed to tell & show me everything and grateful when I told him he was an artist, as indeed he was. His product, sold for about 60 - 70 cents is really a work of art — handmade paper & bamboo. (Why are the Japanese adopting our ugly metal umbrellas?) He knew he was an artist & he was proud of his art. While we talked the house filled up with wondering neighbors.

After that a little more walk and then we bought some fruit & boarded our train for a long dirty overnight trip in a 3rd class car where I was bitten by fleas but managed to sleep pretty well. We arrived next morning before dawn at Shingu & went to the house of Kyosan's uncle Dr. Yamagata.

No more now. My car will be here any minute. In Sendai for 3 days.   Farmy

---

Oct 31, 1950 (postmarked Nov 1)   *Exploring the Kii Coast*
JW in Shingu to Cambridge, MA

Dear Anne & Jeff — I mailed you a letter this morning in which I tried to bring you up to date on my doings without much success. There is one long gap which I still have to fill in, which covers the trip to the Kii Penninsula in Sept with Kurahashi.

As I wrote you, we took the train to Shingu, where we arrived in the dark of the very early morning & made our way to Dr. Yamagata's house & little private hospital. The whole city of Shingu, having miraculously escaped the war, was completely destroyed by fire & earthquake soon afterwards. Most of the present buildings are therefore somewhat of the nature of shacks. The Y's house was more or less like the rest. There was a small hospital building in front & house behind. It is a gross exaggeration to speak of it as a hospital. There is room for only 2 or 3 patients. There are two nurses who also do part of the housework for Mrs. Yamagata.

To Kyoshi's gentle call there was finally the answer of footsteps and we were welcomed by Mrs Y just as dawn was coming. We were glad enough to have a hot bath in a wooden box tub & change our clothes before breakfast. Mrs Y was the cousin of Kyoshi's mother. She was friendly & delightful & evidently very fond of Kyoshi. Her family were important people & had lived in Nachi & Katsuura. The grandfather had been head man (mayor) of Katsuura & had owned a whaling vessel. Dr. Y (born in Hiroshima) had come as a young doctor to Nachi after graduating from Kyoto Med Sch & had married there. He was a pleasant man of about 60. We all talked for some time after breakfast & then I went to sleep. After lunch Kyoshi & I explored the city until supper time.

Shingu lies at the mouth of the Kumano River, one of the large swift rivers of Japan, down which we had hoped to come by raft if the typhoon had not changed everything & made it impossible to complete our trip across the mountains. The city is on a shelf of low land between the shore and a backing of steep hills and mountains. On rough nights we could hear the rote of the waves on the sandy beach a couple of miles away from our house. I suppose I was the only foreigner in the city of 100,000 or so. Certainly the post office people had no trouble in reaching me at the RR station just as I was boarding the train after I had left an obscure telegram for them to send.

Next day we took lunch & sketching things & made our way 10 miles or so NE along the shore by local bus. There we descended & walked along a precipitous path on the face of the cliffs. We met some oyster fishermen & a diver with his wife & child. The diver, a fine bronzed youth in his loin cloth, gave us some big conchs to eat raw, which we accepted. I stopped for a sketch — one of the few I have had a chance to try — & then we made our way back to the long beach where the boats were hauled up & nets were drying. Tiny children were playing unwatched at the edge of the line of rather large breaking waves. A diving fishery was working at the corner between cliffs & beach, and we too went in swimming.

Just then we noticed a fishing boat taking on passengers. A plank had been run out to the bow from the beach which gave precarious access to the boat as it rose & fell to the waves. A number of men & women were going aboard, evidently bound somewhere along the coast, and we saw fire pots being taken on & tea kettles. Suddenly the idea occurred to me that we might go too & K, after making inquiries, said the boat was bound for some isolated villages approachable only by sea but that it was very uncertain how we could get back. But we threw caution to the winds, gathered up our clothes & went aboard as we were with only our loin cloths, which are quite a respectable costume here.

It was a fine trip past some towering headlands forming deep bays until we got to a little village with a well sheltered stone quayside. We went ashore & followed the boatman to his house. We in turn were followed by a long trail of women & children, dumbfounded at the sight of us strangers. When we opened our maps in the boatman's house to inquire about places & paths, they crowded round us so that we had hardly light to see.

At last we discovered that there was a footpath leading over the next mountain to the deep bay beyond & that, from there, we might walk inland along another path to a road where there might be a bus to our point of embarkation. So we decided on that, not really caring whether we got home that night or not. As we cleared the village, we passed a school & there was an uncontrolled rush of students to the windows to have a look at the strangers & the white man, and the teachers followed. Our path led up through the terraced rice fields & then into the woods. It was only a passage between the villages and was paved with rough stones. Just before we entered the woods, we turned back to look at the village we had just left with the sun sparkling on the water beyond & then, farther off still, the next headland.

It was perhaps 1 1/2 hrs walk to the divide. And our path was just the way a road should be between two villages: narrow, cool, shady & worn only by feet. At the divide we drew in our breath at the sight of the next bay, lying dark blue & brilliant, the sun being behind us, and ringed about by precipitous mountains, I suppose it was 15 miles across, with many arms into which we could not see, and with little sprinklings of fishing towns here & there. We sat for some time looking at it and telling ourselves that we would not give any thought to where we slept that night. Then we started down the path, which was rougher & steeper on that side and by and by came out on some sunny terraces where tangerines wre growing.

At the sea's edge we came upon the village & a boatyard where we made enquiries & had a look at a big ceremonial boat which was sheltered there. The people urged us to spend the night where we were but we decided to go on over the next mountain to the bay beyond. As we walked along the quayside path we were surrounded by a rabble of children, very polite but making all sorts of comments on us. When we stopped to buy some fruit, they stopped too. It was like the flies which surround one in the far North and form a traveling environment.

The path to the next village was somewhat longer & less steep in the nigh [sic] side. It also led through the woods and, as we toiled up, we were met by the wives of some charcoal burners tripping down as easily as could be, each with a 60 lb bag of charcoal on her head. They are fine specimens except for their teeth and make our women seem very slouched, soft and pulpy by comparison, and white like a plant grown in the dark.

At the next divide we had the view of an even wider & deeper bay but some of the exhilaration of the first sight of such things had cooled. It was by now quite late in the day & we hurried to get down off the mountain. Just as we reached the village below, a small cargo steamer hove to 300 yds off shore while a boat was sculled out to put some people aboard. We tried to hail them, for we wanted to go almost anywhere in our mood, but it was too late. And I am glad it was. So we walked the crazy little street of the village, again watched & followed, stopping to buy some more fruit. There was a delightful cool grove of monstrous old trees belonging to a shrine on a point jutting out into the bay & we stopped there to enjoy the last of the sun coming down through the branches. The boles of some of the trees must have been 8 ft through.

As we emerged from the grove and were contemplating the deep arm of the bay between us & the next village, we saw a boat with just 2 men in her just shoving off. So we hailed them and asked if we might get in. They were most polite in taking us aboard and, after stopping to look at some of their fish pots, they set out with the big scull oar to cross the arm. It was about sunset when we reached the other side but we were bound we would go on. The twilight was long. And so we continued for another hour & 1/2 round the next promontory to two villages at the head of the centre arm of the bay. There we found two tiny inns. We made enquiries &, with our usual following, inspected both. It was dark by now. We decided on the one nearest the water & were shown in & upstairs to a nice open room where we put on yukatas. Before supper we each had a steaming hot bath in the dark little wooden box tub. Afterwards our individual lacquered tables were brought in laden with miso soup, sashimi and all the most delicious fish.

Outside our audience was gathered on a high bank where they could look into the window. It added to their evening's amusement to have something to look at in their stroll along the water's edge. What a warmth & wealth of life! Fishing, talking, strolling; mothers or grandmothers holding their young over the quayside before bed. After supper we put on getas and went clomping up the cobbled streets. Most of the shoji were closed now but, instead of life itself, we had the shadow play of what went on behind, the figures all made very large by the diverging light.

Next morning we were up before dawn to catch the little steamer that ran back along the coast. It was raining & we were escorted under big Japanese umbrellas to the little inlet where we and some other passengers got into the small boat to be sculled out to where the steamer lay to for us. Two or three men at the sculls sent us along at a great rate & we were on board & away in no time at all. The trip back showed us the rugged coast in quite a different guise (for it was now light.) It took only about 3 hrs to get back to the beach were we had been swimming the day before but it was rough, for another typhoon was in the offing, and I was nearly sick. Kyosan is a good sailor.

We were back in Shingu, where the good Yamagatas were waiting for us, in time for lunch. But directly afterwards we set out in one of the river boats to go up the Kumano River. They are very long shoal-draft boats with a little house running almost the full length & driven by an airplane propellor at the stern. They make good time & there is no danger to an underwater screw in running aground. We spent that night at a side stream in a small inn where there is a hot spring right in the bed of the river. We were the only guests.

No more now. I must meet Tanaka to see some Chinese paintings. I am afraid I bore you both with too many details. Anne! Do write Tanaka's daughter. She longs to hear from you.   Farmy

Nov 4, 1950 (postmarked Nov 6)

Presents
JW in Kyoto to Cambridge, MA

Dear Anne, I am sending you separately a roll of ukiyoe — about 2 doz. They are not valuable. They are copies. Some poor, some fairly good & made long ago, of famous pictures. I wish you would give one each as an Xmas present to: Aunt Susan, Unlce Harry & Aunt O, the Demoses, Nan, the Edsalls, Cousin Ethel, Holly.

The rest are for us. You & Jeff may want some framed for your rooms. The original good prints are worth hundreds of dollars. These give something of the effect of the originals. There are two modern prints with the others.

I cannot send any presents for Xmas but will bring some things with me. I also send some Xmas cards etc. from some friends here who gave them to me for my daughter. I bought today two very nice pieces of old gold lacquer of middle or later Edo period. One a writing case [this was later stolen from Cambridge] & one a lunch box. I was given a handsome screen, which was a little embarrassing, by the University of Kyoto in recognition of my lectures. (10,000 yen, but not so much as it sounds.) This was instead of an object because they felt I had very marked tastes & I decided to use it [the money] in this way on something quite characteristic of Kyoto. Tanaka helped me pick it out.

Lots of love, Farmy.

Write again soon. I have only had one letter since college opened.

Nov 12, 1950

"Nymphs" on Kumano River
JW in Osaka to Cambridge, MA

Dear Anne & Jeff, I must try to finish my account of my trip to the Kii Penninsula in Sept. I am way behind my schedule & going backwards every day.

I told you how I Kyoshi & I started up the Kumano River in a

"Propellor boat" (driven by the airplane propellor) to spend the night at a little hot spring & then go on. The hot spring was a tributary of the main river & now it was a different boat into which we changed which took us on from the junction of the two streams, one very clear, the other turbid, which came together in a turmoil of waters. There were lots of river boats, very beautiful, long and narrow, driven by poles and sculls which ferried people across at this important point. (Our own boat was simply one of these with a house and engine.)

On the way up the tributary we came upon a very beautiful sight, all the more so from being encountered in that wild mountainous setting. It was a fleet of river boats, under sail, trying to make their way up against the current before a leading wind. They were deeply laden, each with a crew of four or five watermen, local to the river. They were just getting underway as we passed them and some had not yet set their sails. They were strange beautiful things, rather more like birds than boats or at any rate like some kind of river beings. I was deeply humiliated at doing them the indignity of passing them in the propellor boat. Their sails are made of separate strips of light canvas set on a yard which is hoisted to the masthead. The tall mast is well stayed when mounted but is taken down when not in use. The yards, as I recall, had braces and the sails bow lines and sheets. I left them with the same feelings with which I might have passed a company of nymphs. I am told the sails have more effect when subdivided in this way. The knowledge of this principle long antedates that recognized in our own parachute spinnakers with their central hole.

In the later afternoon we arrived at another division of waters and again made our way, this time on foot, up the lesser stream. After about a mile of walking up the gorge of a clear crystal stream, we came to a place where the valley opened out and there was our inn. The river was deep just above it but directly in front it was shallow and overhung by a breath of steam from the volcanic springs which bubble up through the bed. We mounted to our room (we were the only travelers) and after tea & cakes went down for a hot bath in the spring. It was partially closed off from the river by a few stones piled in a ring. The water was frightfully hot & the servants came down to help us open the barrier to regulate the temperature. It was delightful to alternate a swim in the cool deep pool with ...[bottom line torn off]...

sunbathing. Other parts of the river were supplied by springs and we came upon warm pockets, marked by hanging vapor, as we roamed up & down the river.

After the swim we put on yukatas and had a good supper & then went for a walk up the valley in the dark. In many places the country people were bathing in similar walled off pools to the one we had used. Then to bed and the next day up at sunrise to return to the junction of the two main streams and take the boat up the Kumano itself, through the gorge known as the Doro. It was drizzling and two of the girls from the hotel walked down part way with us to our point of embarkation to hold umbrellas over us. But the rain stopped by and by, before we got to the gravelly spit where the propellor boat would nose in.

As we waited, what should I see but the same fleet of river boats of the day previous, their masts down, being laboriously towed and poled upstream by their crews. The men had long ropes and were bent double under the pull. They were well in on our side and I ran out over a wide expanse of river gravel to intercept them as they passed. Kyoshi joined me. The boatmen were proud of their profession, which is a vanishing one, thanks to the evil offices of the propellor boats. And they were much pleased at my admiration of their boats. Strong small men, they were, shod with straw shoes, some with umbrella hats and all with the ancient dress. They paused to tell of their river life and explained how they worked, even in mid-winter, half the day up to their thighs in water. Then one of them made a very sad and beautiful remark. "Yes," said he mournfully, "we are a vanishing people, like the wild geese." And, indeed, there is much in the comparison with thse rare and departing birds. Then he said good bye and they struggled on and I got into the propellor boat with a sense of contamination and remained a long time thinking of the boats and the wild geese.

(I must go off to the university now, but will continue later.)

On the way up the Doro, K[yoshi] & I sat in front with the pilot to have a better view. Light rain squalls passed but we preferred getting wet to having our sight of the gorge interfered with. The cliffs became steeper & steeper and more and more fantastic. The river was very swift, far too swift for any rafts to come down, owing to the run-off after our friend the typhoon, but very clear. It was much like an Oriental landscape painting of the most imaginative kind and the rain & mist added greatly to its character. One cannot understand Oriental landscapes properly without having seen the real thing in the East.

We went to the end of the route where we ate our cold rice and fish & then came back in the same boat. Our speed down was very great but we stopped a number of times below the main gorge to pick up local passengers. There were of course no stagings or wharves but the boat ran up against the banks where they were boldest. We passed two white monkeys in the overhanging woods on the port side and there were many charcoal burners' huts and kilns to be seen.

We got back in time for a good sukiaki at the Yamagatas'. Another typhoon was threatening but it was reported to have paused in its tracks a few hundred miles offshore. We could hear the roar of the sea on the beach rising higher and, after supper, decided to walk to the shore to have a look. Mrs. Y[amagata] guided us through the dark lanes & streets with a flashlight to her brother's house which was very close to the water. There was no wind to speak of but some fairly heavy seas were breaking on the sands in the darkness. We went back for a call on the brother & then home to bed.

Next day the typhoon was still keeping people guessing & it threatened rain. But we decided to take a boat some way up the river & walk over the mountains to the sacred Nachi Waterfall, the subject of the great Yamatoye painting in the Nezu collection. It poured cats & dogs on the way up the river but, in our day's walk over the hills, we only got a drenching once. We followed small footpaths from one village to another, crossing several saddles, descending into some steep valleys & finally passing over a kind of upland natural rock garden of great boulders surrounded by terraced rice fields to the main divide. It was completely isolated territory & the houses just as they have been from time out of mind. The old Japanese farm house is very beautiful in shape & texture and accessory stone work. (No one with a scrap of feeling ought to tolerate concrete for one moment where stone exists. I have always hated its miserable color & texture. Why do we, the richest people in the world, allow the use of concrete & deny ourselves the joy of stone? I suppose most of us neither see nor care.)

After crossing the Nachi River we finally arrived abut 3:30 P.M. at the falls. They are about 400-500 feet high, small as to volume but fine as to form. They are surrounded at the bottom by a grove of primeval cedar trees. They were much swollen by the rains & the spray was blowing hard under the force of the wind. There is a shrine nearby. We stayed for a time & then caught the local bus which took us down to the shore, where the little railway line runs past as far as Shingu. The wind was onshore & rising & the sea was quite rough. All the boats had been hauled way up in anticipation of the typhoon. I had just time for a swim before the train came. Kyoshi would not for he considered it too cold. (It was very warm actually.)

When we got back to Shingu we found the Kumano [River] was in semi-flood. Next morning we went to look at it before taking a train down to Shionomisaki, the southernmost cape of Honshu. There we watched the surf & had lunch, sheltering between the squalls in a house where we got tea & cakes. On the way back we stopped at the old whaling town of Katsuura where many boats had come in for shelter from the impending storm, which had everyone guessing. Many of the smaller boats had been hauled right up into the streets. We went out to a little island forming one side of the harbor & climbed to the top to look out over the wild ocean. The sense of the coming storm (which in the end never came but turned off to Kyushu) gave it a dramatic effect. Then we went into a cave where there was a hot spring bath at the threshold of the sea & finally back to Shingu by train.

Next day we set off for Osaka, via Shirahama, where there is a biological station. We were escorted to the station by Mrs Yamagata & the farmer & his wife who supply them vegetables. He had come to give me a present of early persimmons because I had written a card for him to his uncle in California & his wife carried our bags in her cart. Did I tell you of his remark about his uncle's daughter, whose photograph in wedding dress he had seen? "And would you believe it," said he, "she was dressed in mosquito netting?"

By now the typhoon had left us & it was bright again. It was an all-day's trip, with 3 hrs out at Shirahama, to Osaka where we were met by Akabori, Nitta & Ichihara & I was billeted in the Osaka Hotel. Kyoshi went on to Tokyo.

This letter will reach you about Thanksgiving. Give my love to everyone at Walpole [N.H.] I only wish I could be with you. But this stay in Japan is being a most enlarging experience for me & has opened my eyes to so much that I cannot complain.   Farmy

---

Dec 3, 1950
                                                    Fukuoka
                                        JW in Fukuoka to Cambridge

Dear Anne,   This is only a note to tell you of my arrival at Fukuoka after two weeks of walking and traveling with Kyoshi in Shikoku [sic.] — a wonderful trip.

This is the take off point for the front, which is only about 1 hr away I suppose for the fast fighters, & a very active air base & hospital centre. It is not an attractive city but I expect to have an interesting time here. I give 4 lectures & then set off for more walking (after a stop at Nagasake) in S. Kyushu with Okhi. After that, two social weeks in Tokyo & then I am off to Bangkok & India unless an intensification of the war forbids.

This is not a real letter but only a request that you send me the name of yr friend in Damascus [Tamsin Giles] whom it would be amusing to meet if she is there. Write return air mail & I shall get it before I leave.   Farmy

---

Dec 4, 1950
                                        Thinking of Christmas
                                    JW in Fukuoka to Cambridge, MA

Dear Anne, I have just received this Xmas card from my good friend Sugawara [of Nagoya University] enclosed in one of his letters. Please be sure to acknowledge it at it means a lot to the Japanese. They are very friendly to U.S. & also most polite. I hope you have found time to write to the Tanaka girl. When I saw her in Kyoto she was disappointed not to have heard from you.

I wrote you a brief line yesterday & will say no more, except that there is much feeling among the Japanese about Truman's remarks about using the bomb. [in Korea?] There is nothing I believe the

Russians would rather have us do — It would show what we have, raise great opinion against our inhumanity & completely justify them [the Russians?] in using theirs.   Farmy

---

Christmas Day, 1950   *Last Days in Tokyo*
              JW at Imperial Hotel, Tokyo, to Cambridge, MA

Dear Anne & Jeff, Merry Christmas! This is a curious place for me to pass it but I find the Westernized Japanese of Tokyo have taken to it [Christmas] like ducks to water. I got a letter from each of you several days ago, which was a great pleasure. I do not expect any more before I leave here Jan 4.

My itinerary is as follows:

Jan 4	Arr Bangkok (via Hong Kong) 6:15 P.M.
Jan 11	Lv Bangkok
Jan 11	Arr Calcutta
Jan 16-23	New Delhi
Jan 23-26	Karachi
Jan 26-31	Istanbul
Jan 31 - Feb 1	London

(I must see the Turners in the Millbank Gallery if I can)

Feb 2	Arr Washington
Feb 4	Arr Boston

But I may change the times of the later part of the trip slightly. I am longing to see you both & hear & tell of many things.

My letters have collapsed but I must bring the records up to date when I get back, Things have become more & more busy & in some ways more & more interesting: long walking trips, many dinners, weddings, bull fights, Noh plays, lectures, experiences in boats etc.

I will illustrate by my doings in Tokyo day before yesterday: Breakfast 7:15. An interview with two reporters. Then met Prof. Akabori from Osaka. Drove down towards Yokohama to be shown the Ajinomito factory. To a midday dinner given by the president & managing director of it. To a dance given for me by the people at the

Institute for Physical & Chemical Research of Tokyo Univ. at Komba. At the end of it I had the experience of being tossed in the air. You would have laughed to see me.

Well, I will say no more now, except that I am longing to see you both. Give my love to the family.

I am glad you (A.C.W.) saw Tamamushi. His son was at the dance. Farmy

---

Jan 4, 1951 (Postmarked Jan 15 Calcutta)   *An Ice Cream Farewell JW enroute to Bangkok, to Cambridge, MA*

Dear Anne & Jeff, It is hard to realize that my stay in Japan is over. And I feel unhappy that so much of it — more than half — is still unrecorded in my letters or anywhere else.

It was the last half that in many ways was the richest. Certainly my friendships ripened and became more satisfying as time passed. But life became so full that it was hard to find any time for letters. For example, in the last stay in Tokyo I lunched & dined out at almost every meal, or had people in. And a lot of friends from the provinces turned up in town.

The night before I left I had an interesting dinner with Compton Pakenham, chief of the bureau for Newsweek in Tokyo. He is an upperclass Englishman, I suppose nearly 60 years old. His father was naval attache at the British Embassy in Tokyo & he grew up there & speaks Japanese fluently. But he went to Harrow and was there with Nehru. I met him under rather curious circumstances about 6 weeks ago in Nagoya. I was given a large suite of rooms there in the Air Force headquarters — bathroom, dressing room, bedroom, parlor & entrance hall & wash room— which I occupied in solitary grandeur for nearly a week. Then the weather closed in and all the planes were grounded, among others that taking Pakenham to the Korean front. For lack of space, they put him in with me.

At first I thought him a most unprepossessing man — enormously fat & plethoric — and when we met in the morning I was inclined to be cool. But he was evidently a most unusual person and, as we talked, I became more & more taken by him. He had much to say about Korea & the occupation & we sat chatting for a long time. He hates MacArthur, whose egotism he said was "revolting," and illustrated [it] by many accounts of his press conferences. He had been refused permission to reenter Japan by G.H.Q. a year or so ago because of unflattering remarks he had made about MacA but after a showdown, which involved appeal to the President [Truman] himself, [Packenham] had won out. We found ourselves in close agreement on many things about Japan & when we parted he thrust into my hand the book by Sir George Sansom, now at the British Embassy in Tokyo, which is most interesting, "Japan and the West." You should read it. A little heavy perhaps & trying to imitate Gibbon but full of ideas. Pakenham wanted me to meet Sansom but I had no time.

So we agreed to meet in Tokyo as we parted that afternoon, when I left for Osaka & he stayed behind to wait for weather. The first chance was the night before I left when Packenham was to dine with me. I also invited the Indian minister, M. Chettur, but in the end he turned out to be sick so Packenham & I dined alone. Next day Chettur told me Pakenham had said some very sarcastic things about India, so perhaps it is just as well they did not meet. I wondered whether that was the nature of his sickness.

Packenham turned up all dressed for dinner in a boiled shirt & in a dinner jacket of very long dimensions. We went to the cocktail lounge first & discussed all sorts of things so that we did not sit down to dinner until nearly 9. He told me about his showdown over permission to return to Japan when he went to see Truman, whom he said did not seem to have "the foggiest notion what things were all about." He told a rather Rabelaisian story, quoting T[ruman.] In T's office there was a huge map of the world and, pointing to it, T said "They come in here and talk for two hours. They tell me there is pressure here and pressure there! and trouble in another spot. I listen until they have finished and then I go upstairs and have a p___ and forget it all."

A very interesting idea of Packenham's was that the Chinese went into Korea, as and where they did, to keep the Russians out. He does not believe the Chinese act at the direction of Moscow. No doubt each of the two tries to use the other. (I believe it is a mistake to assume that, because China is "Communist," she is bound to be our the partner of Russia.) But P. felt the situation in Korea was very bad.

Earlier in the P.M. I had had a goodbye call from Larry Bunker, who is I suppose as close (perhaps closer) to MacArthur as or than anyone else & is his aide. I like hearing Bunker's ideas because I am sure they are MacArthur's, though they do not greatly impress me. Bunker seemed to feel it was a grave question whether, under present conditions, we could stay in Korea or not. I wish I could have gotten together with Packenham in Tokyo sooner, for he is an engaging man.

Yesterday was my last day and I had a good many things to do. I was up at 6:15 for packing, then went to the Air Office to see about having things shipped back, then to my own office to say goodbye & have a long talk with Jack O'Brien & Bowen Dies [?]. The former had recently come back from Bangkok and loaded me with letters to embassy & govt. people which are almost too much of a good thing but it will make life easy. In order to give me a good entree, he recalled a package which was to be sent to the U.S. Embassy in the diplomatic pouch and gave it to me to carry in my bag. Typical of his shrewdness. He [O'Brien] is incomparably more astute than most generals & I gather a good soldier. He has written a book about the use of artillery in the last war, which was his job.

After that I had a short time with the Indian minister to get some letters for New Delhi etc & then met Kyoshi with whom I went off to spend some of my money on Jap. things. His mother has a friend whose husband was purged & who has now become poor as a result & acts as agent informally for a number of people who want to raise money on their possessions. I bought a picture (a small one) which I liked very much & which I think you will like — a sumi-e (black & white) signed by Sesshu. It may be a forgery but it is, in any case, a very beautiful picture to my mind & has such characteristic brush-work that I (in my ignorance) feel it must be real. I also bought a large, rather gorgeous 6-panel screen of early Edo era (about 1630-1650) by one of the Kanos and a large bronze Chinese vase of Han period.

It was late afternoon when we got back, having had no lunch, so we had a heavy tea in my room. Then I had a call from Gen. Marquat, head of ESS, to ask if I could come over to receive a letter from him in acknowledgment of my services & to say goodbye. It was a fulsome but very nice letter as you will see. He is a funny old man who really does not know what things are about & whose true interest is base-ball.

I hurried back because I had left Kyoshi in my room & also had invited the Miuras with their children to come in for an ice cream party. They were all waiting when I got back & in addition I found I had just missed a call from Admiral Nawa whom I liked greatly & who gave me a wonderful dinner party on New Year's Eve. That was disappointing. He has a most whimsical sense of humor. Kyoshi stayed on and later Mizushima came in for a time. They left late in the evening & I got into bed for a few winks before Bowen Dies & his wife came to pick me up & drive me out to Haneda Field where my plane left at 1:30 A.M. Goodbye Japan! I was relieved to get off but sad to go. About 1/3 ton of stuff will be sent direct by ship, mostly presents, but a good many purchases also. It will be fun opening them with you both when they arrive, probably in March.

Our first stop was Okinawa, a barren place now after the war but I had a glimpse of some of the other Ryuku Islands which looked most tempting. And from the airfield, looking out over the beach where the breakers were rolling in, I could see one of them with its jagged hills.

Since I wrote this I have reached Bangkok where I am sitting in a large airy room in the Trocadero Hotel after a breakfast which included all sorts of tropical fruits. I have my thinnest clothes on for the temperature is that of a fine midsummer's day at home. Soon I shall fare forth.

Hong Kong was spectacular from the air, with many mountainous islands & the sea filled with Chinese junks sailing fast under a brisk wind. China is much more as it used to be than Japan. It made me think of all our family background of China traders to see it all. But I had no time to leave the airport, which is on the water's edge, so I strolled to & fro enjoying the sea breeze & trying to clear my ears until the plane took off once more on the last hop to Bangkok. Much was over the sea & over the clouds but, towards sunset, we were above land & I could look down on a world of uninhabited jungle with bold hills & serpentine rivers. Later, at dusk, I could see some fires of peasants as we approached.   No more now   Farmy

Appendix of Names

Bunker, Col. Laurence: Aide-de-camp to General MacArthur
Dan, Baron: an art figure; son at Misake marine lab
Hamada, Tosiro: Sapporo University rugby player; guide in Hokkaido
Harada, Jiro: Director, National Art Museum
Herrington: director of fisheries for SCAP
Hirata, Count: father-in-law of Yoshiaki Miura, at Nasu
Hayashi: emeritus professor, Imperial University, Tokyo
Kamayama: President, Japanese Council of Science
Kobayashi: obstetrician at hospital on Sado Island
Kodama: chairman Biochemistry Dept., Imperial University, Tokyo
Kurada: Emperor's master of ceremonies under Matsudaira
Kurahashi, Kyoshi: 28-year old biochemist, walking companion
Kurahashi, Takeshi: prof. of drama Waseda U., brother of Kyoshi
Matsudaira, Marquis of: Emperor's grand master of ceremonies
Matsumoto: a Samurai, Imperial rep. at British Coronation
Miura, Reiko: wife of Yoshiaki and daughter of Count Hirata
Miura, Yoshiaki: biochemist Tokyo U., consultant to drug company
Mizushima, Ichiro: physical chemist, ex-dir Sci-Tech Inst. Komba
Muraji: official at marine biology station in Misake
Nagaoka: owner of Kamakura boatyard, uncle of Kurahashi
Nakamura: biochem prof. at Sapporo Univ.; guide to Ainus
Nawa, Baron: Vice Admiral who invented the two-man submarine
Nezu: Pres. Nikko RR, owner of great private art collection
Nishina: Theor. physicist, president of co. doing pure research
O'Brien, Brig. John: Cdr-in-ch Cmnwlth. Forces; Sci. arm of SCAP
Packenham, Compton: bureau chief for Newsweek in Tokyo
Saito: member of the House of Lords & Insurance magnate
Sebold: U.S. Ambassador to Japan
Shimazono: biochemist, Secretary to Niigata University
Shoda: Pres. of a modern yeast co., related to Mizushima
Sugawara: dean of science faculty, Nagoya University
Tanaka: professor at Kyoto University
Tindale: SCAP official involved in civil affairs
Warner, Langdon: curator and lecturer in Oriental Art at Harvard
Yamagata: Dir. small hospital in Shingu, uncle of Kurahashi
Yamaji: director of folk museum outside Tokyo

Appendix of Historical Periods

857-1185 - Fujiwara era - Capitol was Heian (Kyoto)
1185-1333 - Kamakura era - Shoguns, Daimyos, Samurai
1333-1598 - Ashikaga (Muromachi) era
1598-1868 - Tokugwa (Edo) era - Japan closed to the West
1868-1912 - Meiji era - also known as "Meiji Restoration"

Appendix of Words

Ainu - aboriginal people of Hakkaido
Bugaku - traditional music and dance of the imperial court
Daimyo - a provincial ruler
Dotera - an outer robe
Genji, Tale of - 11th century court novel by Lady Murasaki
Geta - wooden clog shoes
Hashi - chopsticks
Kakemono - a vertical scroll painting
Makimono - a horizontal scroll painting
Noh - professional dance drama dating from the 14th century
Obi - a sash worn by men and women
Samurai - a warrior
SCAP - Supreme Command, Allied Powers
Shamisen - a three-striged lute
Shogun - a military ruler of all Japan
Shoji - room dividers or sliding screens
Shrine - represents Shinto (ancestor) worship
Tatami - a woven floor covering of straw
Temple - represents Buddhist place of worship
Tokonoma - an alcove for ornaments
Ukiyo-e - 17th to 19th century woodblock print of everyday life
Yukata - an informal robe, usually worn at home